RETREATS
for the SOUL

RETREATS
for the SOUL

SUSTAINABLE AND STYLISH
HIDEAWAYS AND HAVENS

SARA BIRD &
DAN DUCHARS of
The CONTENTed Nest

RYLAND PETERS & SMALL
LONDON • NEW YORK

Senior designer Toni Kay
Editor Sophie Devlin
Senior commissioning editor Annabel Morgan
Location research Jess Walton
Head of production Patricia Harrington
Creative director Leslie Harrington

Published in 2023 by
Ryland Peters & Small
20–21 Jockey's Fields,
London WC1R 4BW
and
341 East 116th Street
New York, NY 10029

www.rylandpeters.com

10 9 8 7 6 5 4 3 2 1

UK ISBN 978-1-78879-549-4
US ISBN 978-1-78879-511-1

A CIP record for this book is
available from the British Library.

Library of Congress CIP data
has been applied for.

Printed and bound in China

FSC
www.fsc.org

MIX
Paper from
responsible sources
FSC® C106563

CONTENTS

INTRODUCTION

Our retreat spaces are personal, private and peaceful places to nest, nurture and take time out. They offer a chance to escape and take a break from everyday matters. A retreat can be somewhere to discover and potter, take up pastimes and activities or rest and recharge alone or with loved ones.

Nowadays, our busy lives are filled with to-do lists, commitments and calendared events. As a result, it has become even more important that we learn how to step back, disengage and be in the moment. Establishing a place for regular downtime opportunities, days off and breakaway moments is a great way to achieve this. It can be life-enhancing, forge healthier habits and lead to new creative opportunities.

Our vision of these wide-ranging spaces is all about fashioning a unique setting in which to explore your passions, be it a homely hut, a waterside getaway or a remote custom-made smart pod. Some of the retreats in this book were designed from the outset with a purpose in mind, while others have been gradually tailored to suit their owners' changing needs, but they are all inspiring places to sit and daydream.

These places of self-discovery also offer the opportunity to care for our mental and physical wellbeing and connect to nature within an alternative environment. Blurring the boundaries between indoors and out reaps all the benefits of biophilic design. These new surroundings lead to fresh sights and sounds throughout the seasons.

Creating our own sanctuaries also brings the prospect of more mindful and conscientious building and styling in which we strive to be resourceful with materials, mind our ecological footprint and seek out innovative design. Using sustainable ingredients, upcycling and repurposing will add character and authenticity.

In *Retreats for the Soul*, we hope to inspire with inventive ideas for spare-time spaces and bespoke boltholes, whether close to home or further afield. If you are dreaming of your own soulful sabbatical, these remarkable spaces will provide ample encouragement.

1

THE ELEMENTS

STRUCTURES
& MATERIALS

From simple shelters to more complex conversions and new-builds, retreats can take many forms. Even if your ambitions are fairly modest, it is worth taking time to plan the construction with care to ensure the best results.

A retreat should be your very own sanctuary, a place that is soulful and uplifting, whether you are investing in something old and ramshackle or creating from new. This starts with your choice of materials and sustainable and handmade elements can be the key to a welcoming retreat.

Your first consideration, especially if you are converting an existing structure, should be how to reuse the materials already available to you on site. If there is anything that can't be employed in the build, you may find a use for it later in your furniture and fittings. Even if you are starting your build from scratch, you may be able to find much of what you need at local salvage yards. It is so satisfying to give a new lease of life to an existing resource, as well as being more affordable and less harmful to the environment than buying new.

If new materials are required, look for natural and organic options and try to avoid synthetic alternatives. Green oak, slate and stone, sheep's wool, straw, bamboo and cork are all sustainable choices for cladding or insulation. Coppiced wood from fast-growing trees is another great renewable resource. When buying new timber, make sure it comes from FSC-certified sources.

For the DIY-shy, there are many specialist artisan makers who design and construct bespoke builds. From shepherd's huts and eco pods to castaway cabins and luxury lodges, they can source all the parts and deliver skilled finishes and details to create the retreat of your dreams.

NEW FOR YOU

Building a retreat gives us the opportunity to do things differently, learn new skills and use unfamiliar materials (this page and opposite). Artisan techniques can be embraced, old methods revived and new ideas applied to construction and creativity. Thinking outside the box helps us face modern dilemmas: future-proofing our sanctuaries to suit our changing climate, fostering better practices and using mindfully chosen resources.

MIXING MATERIALS

Using a combination of building ingredients can help tailor a design to suit your setting, climate or budget (above). Interesting textures and surfaces that complement one another will bring a unique quality from the outset, which will evolve with age.

BUILDING FOR BETTER

The journey of constructing a retreat can be just as enjoyable as its end use, and attention to the details can bring satisfaction for years to come. Turning familiar materials on their side, as in this gable-end log wall (above), can give them a new look. You can also play with stacking, layering and direction to create bespoke patterns and features. The narrow vertical cladding on this cabin has a sleek and contemporary feel, in contrast with the rustic foundation (right).

RESCUE MISSION

Many reclaimed resources can be repurposed or patched up and made good as part of a characterful retreat, from individual bricks and beams to whole structures – this garden studio is based on an old shed that the owners bought from Ebay. Buying secondhand is a great way to give old building materials a new lease of life. It saves money, lessens our eco footprint and reduces consumption and waste.

OLD & NEW

New and reused materials should be chosen with care, especially if they will be exposed to the elements or experience heavy wear and tear (this page and opposite). Low-VOC paints, oils and wood stains can help to preserve and protect surfaces both inside and out. They may also add colour, texture and pattern or simply highlight the natural grain. On the flip side, allowing materials to weather over time has its own appeal. Consider the beauty of oxidized metal, faded wood, sun-bleached colours and distressed paintwork. There are even tricks that will allow you to speed up the ageing process, such as adding sawdust or cement powder to paint for nubby textures. Other recipes use staples from your cleaning cupboard or pantry. Iron acetate (made by dissolving steel wool in vinegar) will darken raw timber, while a mix of vinegar, salt and eco bleach (also known as hydrogen peroxide) will tarnish metal in minutes.

PALETTES, PAINTS & FINISHES

As well as defining the character of a hideaway space, colours and textures are known to have a significant effect on our mood and can shape our play and pastime experiences.

Be it bold colour blocks, soft glazes or diminutive details that draw the eye, the palette that makes you feel at ease in your personal retreat is determined by your own tastes. Creating a place to pursue a pastime requires a different approach to colour compared with a space to switch off and slow down. Each tone and texture lends its own qualities to the overall scheme.

Paint is at the forefront of environmentally friendly design, with an abundance of brands now offering low-VOC formulas made with natural pigments and careful consideration of the end use of both paints and containers. These paints are ideal for a sustainable sanctuary.

A particular hue might offer a connection to nature or a bold contrast, highlight certain features of the room or bring everything together. You should also consider the type of paint and how it will be used. Applied smoothly, paint can bring a glossy finish that reflects light and offers depth of colour, suggesting newness and polish. Distressed paintwork is more lived-in and will gain further character as it ages.

Paints are also the perfect way to revitalize furniture. A roadside castaway, a vintage find or a piece you already own can be saved from landfill and transformed with a lick of colour that suits your scheme.

Because retreats are not everyday living spaces, they make the perfect blank canvas for a creative palette. Opt for vibrancy, suggest softness, combine complementary colours or keep it simple with a tonal or monochrome look. Anything goes, as long as it makes you feel fulfilled.

FAVOURITE SHADES
A one-colour scheme can be very stylish, but a palette of complementary hues is incredibly versatile (this page and opposite). Different colours can offer an inspiring backdrop, establish zones, highlight attractive features and add personality. They can also set the mood, creating quiet corners or lively shared spaces. Choose shades that are unique to you over trend-led palettes for maximum authenticity.

COLOUR CHAMELEON

Even the most pristine finish will change over time
and begin to show signs of wear (opposite and above).
Protecting exposed surfaces using premium eco-friendly
brands rather than cheaper versions will allow you to
paint once well as opposed to many times. Alternatively,
embrace the maturing process and watch surfaces age
with elegance as they bleach, weather and season.

COMPARE & CONTRAST

Colours and materials are invaluable
for establishing distinct zones in a
retreat. Here, a subtly contemporary
glazed lean-to extension has been
attached to an old wooden cabin (left),
and a treehouse's outdoor shower
features a panel of striking blue-green
tiles (above). A subtle transition can
blur the boundary between old and
new, while a flash of colour can excite
and refresh. There is no firm rule, as
long as the materials are fit for their
intended purpose and situation.

FABRICS & TEXTILES

Adding comfort and colour, shade and screening, pattern and sometimes even gentle swishing sounds, fabrics and textiles are an essential element of any retreat and are sure to imbue it with personality.

Draped over furniture, hung up on the walls or fashioned into fluttering flags and ribbons, textiles soften, protect and enhance all kinds of surfaces. Some are made to weather a storm, others to age beautifully. Used in single sheets or multiple layers, they lend stark and shallow spaces depth and complexity.

Many of the most desirable fabrics come from natural fibres: wool, silk, cotton, hemp and even grasses. These represent thousands of years of craftsmanship. New to the market are cloths made from recycled plastics and plant-based leathers. These have water-resistant qualities that make them incredibly useful for outdoor or coastal settings. Always check the environmental and ethical credentials of your chosen fabrics – those that are certified by Oeko-Tex and Fairtrade represent a more conscious choice.

Upcycling and reusing vintage fabrics can be a fantastic way to commit to sustainable living and cut costs when decorating a retreat. These old textiles can also hold many memories. Hand-me-down weaves and prints, clothing, household linens and soft furnishings can be reworked into items that are both practical and personal. You can gather them over a number of years, hanging and draping a little at a time to make your own space.

Fabrics take us from season to season, too, offering warmth and shade. They help establish a space, whether we use it every day or only from time to time. From the floor to the ceiling and into the outdoors, they are easily portable and endlessly versatile with many applications. These pages offer some inspiration on how to bring them into your retreat.

TAILOR-MADE TRICKS
Fabrics are an easy and inexpensive way to make a space unique (this page and opposite). Heavyweight or floating, starched or soft, they add off-the-roll texture, colour and drama. Perfectly finished hems contribute a certain polish, but raw edges can be equally lovely. Plain textiles are easily embellished with trims and tassels, embroidery and stitchwork or origami-style folds and pleats.

WEATHER & WATER

If your retreat has an outdoor space, such as this kitchen (opposite), you may want your soft furnishings to be water-resistant or quick to dry in case of showers. The same applies to bathrooms (right). Weaves made from recycled plastic bottles are one option, or you can coat fabrics with beeswax for an impermeable finish. Alternatively, use temporary textiles that are easy to bring indoors, such as cushions/pillows (above).

OLD FRIENDS

If you are creating a retreat on a budget, even small pieces of fabric can have a big impact. Here we see a simple velvet cushion/pillow in a Scandi-style bedroom (far left) and an inherited chair newly upholstered in a floral print from Cabbages & Roses (left). Rather than buying new, reusing and repurposing favourite fabrics from clothing or homewares reduces waste and rekindles fond memories of people, times and places.

CREATIVE THINKING

Make sure your shelter is comfortable whatever the season or weather with inviting, restful and layered textiles (this page and opposite). Hang up curtains for cooling shade and privacy, and bring in different textures such as thick wools or lightweight linens. Inexpensive textiles can be used in unusual and surprising ways. Keep doors cosy with clipped-up blankets, reuse rugs as coverlets or even repurpose dust sheets as inexpensive throws.

FURNITURE & FITTINGS

Usually installed for practical reasons, furniture and fittings define a retreat's purpose and how we use the space, both for permanent places and for the more pack-up-and-go.

Furniture is what really makes the difference between a set of walls and a habitable room. Whether a retreat is designed for general relaxation, a particular pastime or work on a side hustle, furniture and accompanying fittings allow us to utilize and realise the rationale for its role in our lives. New or old, well-made furniture unites function and personality in its construction, casting a lived-in feel.

If buying new, consider the ethical and environmental impact of how the piece was made and look for eco-friendly and FSC-certified materials. Choose wisely and think how an item might age over time and how it can be adapted and reused if your needs change in the future. Even if you are on a budget, buying a pricier option once is far better for the pocket and

the planet in the end. Bespoke furniture can be particularly expensive, but even off-the-shelf items can be personalized with a new finish or decorative detail. Simple hacks can be just as soulfully satisfying as buying on-spec styles.

Reusing, recycling or rehoming furniture offers a way to prolong its lifespan without compromising your personal style. This can take many forms: updating something with a new cover or colour, chopping and changing to refit a space or refreshing a hand-me-down brings a sense of fulfilment and continues familiarity. New-to-you pieces usually have their own history of wear and tear, which allows us to relax in their presence without worrying about keeping things pristine. This is wonderful for our wellbeing, too.

PRACTICALLY PERFECT

A retreat's furniture and fittings have to meet a number of requirements depending on the size of the space and how it will be used. Boat design can offer inspiration for clever, adaptable features such as compact or folding furniture, sliding doors and wall-mounted storage, which are just as useful on dry land (above left, left and opposite). Functional fittings for outdoor plumbing are robust and inexpensive (top left).

FIT FOR PURPOSE

Outdoor furniture needs to withstand the
elements unless you have a sheltered place
to store it (this page and opposite). Before
buying new, look inside your home for
furniture that can be weatherproofed. The
hardiest material, which provides the best
value for money over time, is FSC wood
that has been thoroughly treated. Bamboo
and rattan are lightweight alternatives.
Metal furniture is another good long-term
investment if looked after, with wrought iron
being the most durable. Canvas deckchairs
and hammocks can be folded up and
brought inside when not in use.

ALL IN THE DETAILS

The finishing touches and fittings are often what bring a retreat to life, especially when they marry usefulness with character and beauty (this page and opposite). They offer an opportunity to upcycle or put a fresh spin on something you already own, add a touch of humour or house the one-of-a-kind piece you have inherited but have no idea where to put. Always check that vintage and inherited components are working properly before you install them. Old electrical appliances and lights should be rewired and checked for safety – here in the UK this is called Portable Appliance Testing (PAT). Plumbing fixtures can be cleaned up with descaler and installed either flush to the wall or on exposed pipework. Antique wooden furniture and details should be checked for signs of rotting or woodworm, and textiles and upholstery will need to be cleaned to make them ready for their new home.

STORAGE & DISPLAY

Keeping clutter to a minimum is essential in an orderly retreat, but not everything needs to be hidden away – open storage enables you to display a curated selection of treasured items that will lend personality to your space.

Nowadays it is easier than ever to take up new pastimes with associated accessories, all of which need a place to live. A retreat is a natural home for this personal paraphernalia. Storage space is always at a premium, but there is still room for creativity as you consider what should be hidden and what belongs out in the open.

Specialized equipment may require imaginative storage solutions. Made-to-measure shelving can be constructed from found materials such as wooden pallets and boards. Meanwhile, old boxes, crates, cans, pots and jars can be filled with odds and ends. If you don't have space for a dedicated storage room, you could find or make a piece of furniture that has a dual purpose, such as a storage bench. Built-in cabinets can be hidden behind panelling or mounted on the wall above head height.

Always plan for more storage than you think you need and make it fit for purpose from the start. If your retreat is near water and you need to store equipment for boating and water sports, having something that can be hosed down is ideal. Or if you need to protect delicate items, sealed storage offers peace of mind.

The other side of storage is display, through which we can share our interests and hobbies. Boating and boarding, fishing and flower arranging, cookery and crafting all bring an array of items that have their own beauty in spite of their often humble origins. Our collections allow us to engage with our more mindful side, celebrate happy memories and connect with nature. Let's not forget humour, too – if something silly or sentimental brings a smile, it is well worth a place in the spotlight.

CLEVER CORNERS

Ample storage is a requirement in most retreats, whether they are used primarily for guest accommodation or as hobby spaces. Try to keep the floor free of clutter and install hooks and rails on the walls and ceilings instead (opposite). Wire cages are a good choice for bulkier items (top right). Freestanding shelves and hooks are a clever combination (above right), while built-in options can be fitted into odd angles (right).

OFF THE WALL

Painted or panelled walls are the perfect blank canvas on which to arrange and display artwork and decorative objects. Small cupboards and shelves in corners are great for delicate items (opposite top left and above). Narrow racks neatly house bound papers and books (opposite bottom left). Clips, clasps and hangers make for a relaxed way to secure favourite things and allow for frequent updates (opposite top right and bottom right).

LOOK UP

When planning out a smaller space, think about how much of its footprint is going to be taken up with large items of furniture, some of which will have unused headroom that you can repurpose for storage and display (this page and opposite). Wall-mounted shelving and cabinets for keepsakes can be positioned above large cupboards, beds, sinks and more, with no additional floor space required. Having enough storage allows you to keep the things you need close to hand and rearrange your collections as often as you like. Even a trim ledge can support personal effects. Shelves finished in the same colour as the wall recede into the background so that the objects take centre stage. Choosing a different material for the shelves will make them stand out more.

LIGHTING & HEATING

Providing sufficient warmth and illumination allows us to enjoy a retreat at all hours and in every kind of weather, even if it calls for a little creative thinking to reduce our environmental footprint.

Being able to maximize the time you spend at your retreat is always an advantage, whether you go there seeking escape, to socialize or to pursue a hobby. Enough heat and light can make a big difference to your overall experience, whatever the barometer brings. Being mindful of greener energy options can also keep power usage down, along with the associated costs, and will give you the satisfaction of making a more sustainable choice.

Smaller spaces don't take much energy to heat and light, but insulation should be embraced to make resources go further. Suitable natural materials include wool, straw and paper. Extra protection can come from heavy fabrics and tapestries on walls and curtains for windows and doors. In the warmer months, good insulation will also keep your space cool and prevent overheating without the need for costly air conditioning. Thicker walls, shaded southerly windows and limited expanses of north-facing glazing will moderate extreme seasonal temperatures.

When decorating your space, be aware that darker colours absorb warmth and light while lighter ones reflect them. Glossy surfaces such as polished tiles, mirrors, metal and lacquered wood will also bounce light around the room and can make it appear larger.

For efficient, eco-friendly lighting, your best option may be LED bulbs, especially if solar-powered. Choose task lighting instead of overhead light fittings to reduce the amount of bulb use, and on relaxing evenings, candlelight rather than ambient light is both eco-friendly and atmospheric.

WARM WELCOME
One of the most important things to consider when creating a retreat is how to make it inviting and comfortable. Having a source of heat allows you to use your new space for longer. Warming oneself by a cosy fire triggers contentment and watching the flames is a relaxing experience (this page and opposite). If fires are not permitted where you live, invest in radiators instead for a smoke-free solution.

ILLUMINATING DETAILS

Lighting in a retreat comes in all shapes and sizes, some discreet while others are valued for their texture, style, material and decorative qualities (this page and opposite). They can inspire and add to the overall look of the interior, introduce an element of fun or be part of a bigger collection of discerning designs. When lit, they establish an atmosphere of peaceful intimacy or full-on party mode both indoors and out.

MINDFULNESS & WELLBEING

Representing a place where we can take the time to tune out, rest and reset, a retreat is a chance for us to fulfil our sensory and psychological needs via thoughtful touchpoints.

Whether a distant destination in the back of beyond or a close-to-home haven just a step away from everyday life, no matter where a retreat is located it can bring a restorative sense of wellbeing with the aid of a few simple design ideas.

Using organic building and decorating materials can tie us holistically to the natural world and particularly to the local landscape. Eco-friendly and reclaimed finishes have charming irregularities that make them especially pleasing to the touch. When integrated into the look and feel of a space, these grounding features allow us to let go of stress and unwind for a moment or more.

Biophilic design presents many benefits to the psyche. A window on the wild, colours from the coast or countryside, houseplants and foraged finds all bring us closer to the natural world. Botanical elements establish a close connection to nature.

Make sure to consider all your senses. Create a space for sound indoors and out, perhaps the rustle of a cooling breeze, the gentle lapping of waves or the flow of running water. Natural scents from plants, candles and incense trigger memories and create a soothing or uplifting atmosphere as required. Frequently inexpensive, these small details are a wonderful way to set the scene.

The best kind of retreat allows you to enjoy the experience from the moment you step inside, so think through all the essentials ahead of time. Make your retreat easy to maintain, clean and protect, and it will help you to slow down and press pause on our busy world.

INNER PEACE
The chance to engage directly with nature outdoors is one of life's luxuries (this page and opposite). A retreat enables us to indulge all our senses and experience something different to the norm when set free in the fresh air. Watching the wildlife, being in contact with the climate and perceiving all the scents, sights and sounds immediately brings biophilic benefits. Making time and space for this brings balance to our core.

BETTER LIVING

One of the best aspects of a retreat is the chance to try different activities or bring new habits into our everyday lives. These refreshing encounters are there to be enjoyed and can be the simplest of things: a lazy lie-in, a dawdled day, warming in the sun or a crisp nip outside (this page and opposite). Or a retreat can be a safe haven away from routine, where hobbies are practised or friends are entertained. The benefits of having another place to explore our interests are life- and soul- enriching.

2
THE RETREATS

CLOSE TO HOME

BELOW
Positioned in a sunny spot in view of the
house, the summerhouse is an inviting
sight. With the doors flung open and
flowers and flags flapping in the breeze,
it beckons to Tamsyn and her family to
come and spend a little time here.

THREADS
of life

A lifelong love affair
with brocante and vintage
textiles has given Tamsyn
Morgans's summerhouse
a laid-back and lived-in feel
thanks to her ever-changing
vintage collections, which
have found a comfortable
home in this Norfolk
garden sanctuary.

Offering a slice of calming countryside in the
middle of suburbia, photographer and stylist
Tamsyn Morgans's soulful summerhouse is
a place where she can mindfully unwind and
express her creativity. It was installed in the
garden in 2014 just after a family move and
serves as an extension of her home. Tamsyn's
personal style is the common thread that unites
both spaces and there is an easy flow between
the two. Homewares can be brought in and out
with sympathetic ease, but the summerhouse
still has its own identity and role for the family.

The short walk from terraced/row house to
summerhouse, along a winding path through
the garden, is a mindful journey that encourages
you to clear your head, disengage from work
and tune out the static noise of everyday life.

ABOVE
Displaying Tamsyn's
collections has presented
opportunities for upcycling.
Her favourite blue-and-white
ceramics and mustard pots
are arranged on secondhand
shelves, which she has
simply refreshed with some
leftover white paint.

OPPOSITE
A cosy corner has been
created with an old sofa from
the main house. To make it
fit the space, the arms and
back had to be removed, so
it is now more of a daybed.
A quilt and some cushions/
pillows complete the look.

The path leads you to a place of peace and calm that has been designed for relaxation. For Tamsyn, the summerhouse represented a blank canvas. It needed personality and authenticity, which she has been able to provide in abundance thanks to her fondness for preloved objects.

Taking inspiration from buildings created using reclaimed architectural details, Tamsyn has brought this look to life on a budget- and build-friendly manner, for example by leaning old window casements and panes against the plain walls and modern windows. These non-fixed fabrications can be moved at a whim and updated along the way. It's an easy-to-emulate styling trick, which adds history and texture to a new-build structure as well as being eco-friendly.

To complement the old windows, Tamsyn has cleverly brought together a selection of landscape paintings and prints to decorate the walls and create a picture-window effect. Offering storyboard scenes and faux views of her favourite places to be, these artworks bring idyllic rural, woodland and even beach vistas to her landlocked retreat and help her to feel connected to the outside world. The biophilic benefits of bonding with nature are well known, and this suburban summerhouse provides a masterclass in reaping the rewards of both city and country living.

THIS PAGE
Packed with decorative detail, the summerhouse features many of Tamsyn's favourite things. There are blooms from the garden (bottom left), pictures of favourite views (top left), collected textile crafts (bottom right) and even her own makes, such as the delightful row of recycled lace and embroidery flags (top right). Each one offers an insight into Tamsyn's style and the little things that make her happy. They are a delightful example of how to create a soulful, uplifting sanctuary.

OPPOSITE
Tamsyn was keen to create a unique setting, but without any difficult DIY tasks. Instead, she has introduced elements that are easy to install and move around, for an interior that shifts with the seasons. Painting the walls a pale colour has created the ultimate blank canvas for items to lean up against, hang down from or drape across. Buckets and baskets host ever-changing displays of flowers and more.

THIS PAGE
Tamsyn has used a pale hue to create a peacefully uniform backdrop across not just the walls but also the ceiling, window casements, furniture and even decorative shelving and moving elements such as these shutters. Finishes are distressed, washed out or worn rather than matching, smooth and immaculate, which makes them easier to layer up, move around and dress up or down. Against the neutral decor, Tamsyn's colourful and decorative collections stand out and draw the eye.

FAR LEFT & LEFT
A major fan of vintage wares, Tamsyn has dedicated her retreat to things that show wear and have already enjoyed a previous life. Every scuff and scrape brings charm, character and individuality.

BELOW
The summerhouse is a joyful sight in the garden, whether in use as an extension of Tamsyn's home or simply as part of the landscape. In winter, she dresses the exterior with lights and decorations.

Nature and the seasons have also influenced the evolution of Tamsyn's beloved collections, which are arranged according to the weather or just a whim. Pretty ceramics, glassware and filigree decor jostle for space, while humble paint cans, pots and jars make a handsome display in spite of their everyday origins. Tamsyn takes a considered and sustainable approach to collecting, so any items she no longer wants are passed on to friends and family or donated to charity rather than thrown away.

Despite the 'summerhouse' label, Tamsyn and her family use this space from early spring until the first frosts of autumn. To make up for the lack of central heating, they rely on candles, lanterns and cosy blankets in the cooler months. Throughout the year, fabric offcuts, old linens and other textile remnants draped over furniture and fittings soften hard edges and create the most beautiful interplay between light and shade. The homely textiles also provide noise insulation and offer ruffling and rustling sounds of their own as they flicker and float in the breeze.

Creating her very own retreat and spending time here has been a healing experience for Tamsyn for personal reasons. It is part of the ebb and flow of her everyday life, as a space for entertaining and a soulful sanctuary. This little summerhouse is a truly captivating corner that offers a warm welcome in all seasons.

The cabin is positioned to create a neat L-shape with the workshop on the right. A deck has been constructed to extend the footprint and create an outdoor living space. This inviting additional seating and dining area has been planted with scented and sculptural shrubs and succulents, which provide interest and fragrance throughout the changing seasons.

RIGHT
Fold-away furniture is brought out onto the deck during the warmer months. This vintage cafe-style table and chairs are a charming and classic option with a slimline profile for easy, space-saving storage.

INSIDE *out*

Sometimes a retreat is born out of necessity, as in the case of this cabin on the Isle of Wight. After going open-plan in their home, owners Helen and David chose to build an additional room in the garden as a self-contained retreat.

With a simple plan in mind, Helen and David approached Dave Coote and Atlanta Bartlett of Pale & Interesting, who have designed and built a number of cabins over the years. Helen and David's wish list included places to sleep, wash and make tea as well as plenty of storage. With a little creative thinking, Dave and Atlanta were able to bring this vision to life.

ABOVE LEFT
Homely and heartfelt touches take pride of place inside. This chair was a gift from friends and the throw was handmade by Helen's mother.

ABOVE CENTRE
Freshly picked garden flowers often find their way into the cabin, where they provide scent, shape and colour.

ABOVE RIGHT
A folded woollen throw from Cornwall-based Atlantic Blankets adds natural warmth.

The cabin was built using a framework of wooden beams and a tongue-and-groove facade. A truly inspired space-making solution came from some vintage French window shutters sourced by Dave and Atlanta. Cleverly lined up in a row at one end of the main bedroom area, the shutters open to reveal three small chambers: a WC, a storage cupboard and a kitchenette. Although a full internal bathroom wasn't an option for reasons of space, cost and practicality, there is an outdoor shower instead for guests to use while staying in the cabin. The sea views across the English Channel more than make up for the lack of indoor convenience.

The roof is topped with galvanized corrugated iron from the West Sussex-based company Southern Sheeting. This robust material will stand the test of time for years to come, with the added sensory benefit of providing a delightful pitter-patter sound overhead whenever it rains. Inside, the cabin feels light and airy, as the roof space and structure have been left exposed to maximize the ceiling height. The interior has been painted white using an inexpensive trade paint for a classic, timeless finish that is unfussy and easy to maintain.

OPPOSITE
A simple white scheme provides a down-to-earth backdrop for occasional pops of colour and pattern. Humble cottage prints and weaves are seen on checked and striped textiles from Helen's favourite stores and her own collection. Living on an island means that online brocante sellers such as @fabulousvintagefinds on Instagram are an essential resource for tracking down authentic antiques with just a few easy clicks.

The decor is humble and homely, with a perfect partnership of old and new and a good dose of upcycling ingenuity. In addition to the vintage shutters, a sheet of zinc originally bought as a kitchen splashback for the main house has now been repurposed to replace the warped wood on top of an old chest of drawers/dresser.

Reclaimed Victorian floorboards have retained their original patina and finish, which bring a sense of authenticity. Brass taps/faucets were sourced from Queen Victoria's own Isle of Wight home, Osborne House in East Cowes. Even the basin surround is made from Cornish Delabole slate that was left over from the bathroom floor in the house.

LEFT
Helen loved the idea of using reclaimed elements in the build alongside newer pieces, so designers Dave and Atlanta have juxtaposed new tongue-and-groove cladding with Victorian floorboards. The combination of the freshly painted bright white panelling and the scuffed and scratched old wood represents a mingling of past and present.

LEFT
At one end of the main room, a row of vintage shutters cleverly screens a line of practical compartments.

ABOVE & OPPOSITE
Behind the shutters, which open out into the bedroom, each of the miniature 'rooms' feels quite spacious. Seen here is the central kitchen/washroom area. It is simply yet delightfully dressed with an ensemble of homely accessories that includes a mirror, basin, kettle and a few essential condiments.

Bedside tables/nightstands come in the guise of old school desks, found at Bramble & Berry on the Island. These are fantastic space-saving pieces with under-lid storage that keeps clutter to a minimum. Homely gingham curtains hang at the windows and under-counter cupboard. Simple linens on the bed are dressed up with cottage-style cushions/pillows from Fabulous Vintage Finds.

Well-read books and hand-me-downs from loved ones bring fond memories into the space. A Lloyd Loom-style chair was passed on by friends and the papier-mâché goat's head above the bed was a playful gift from the couple's nephew. A liquid-emulsion photograph of seaweed by an artist friend, Marysia Lachowicz, hangs above the chest of drawers/dresser. A colourful patchwork blanket knitted by Helen's mother is a particularly treasured piece. All of these cherished objects add character and warmth.

Visual comforts are paired with the sensory benefits of having nature right on the doorstep. The only sounds come from the rustling birds, the clucking of the neighbours' hens and the local badgers running across the lawn.

OPPOSITE

An outdoor shower is positioned to the rear of the property with side access from the cabin and hot and cold water plumbed in from the main house. Fencing and a few wooden boards have been utilized to make a screen for privacy, but the front section was designed to be not as tall so that anyone using the shower can take in the coastal views.

Warming sun streams into the cabin in the morning, so a table and chairs have been placed on the deck – a lovely spot to ease into the start of the day. The garden setting also provides pretty sights and wafts of fragrance from the lavender and lilac planted just outside. Fresh and dried flowers are brought indoors all year round to connect with the seasons and a small vase of blossom in the spring is admired just much as winter holly or hawthorn.

Although initially intended to serve as a guest bedroom, the cabin now doubles as an office, as a backdrop for dining and even as an alternative bedroom for Helen and David, such is its draw and appeal. Much more than just a functional sleeping space, the cabin has been transformed over time into a soulful retreat on the couple's doorstep.

ABOVE

The furniture on the deck – Adirondack chairs, a log table and a simply crafted breakfast bar – has been arranged to make the most of the panorama. It's an inviting place to sit and look out over the busy shipping lanes of the English Channel.

PERSONAL *place*

Inspired by the need to nurture a new-found hobby, photographer Harriet Thistlethwayte's garden studio in Herefordshire has become a welcome place of respite, where creativity can be fostered in private peace.

A new pastime can bring with it all manner of additional needs and requirements, but it was a private workspace that was highest on the agenda for Harriet Thistlethwayte. After a fulfilling life of bringing up children, she naturally had more time on her hands once they left the fold. At this point, her quietly cultivated enjoyment of floral photography propelled the need for a personal place in which to hone her craft.

Harriet planned to locate her studio in the garden of her Herefordshire home, so her first mission was to find a suitable outdoor building. With an ethos of trying old before buying new, she purchased an existing pine shed on Ebay, which her DIY-savvy husband Thomas then assembled in the garden.

THIS PAGE & OPPOSITE
Sourcing a simple secondhand structure
was an eco-friendly and cost-effective
alternative to buying new. A covered deck
has been added to the front as an additional
area for work or rest. It also offers mindful
benefits, acting as a bridge from her
creative workshop inside to the inspiring
botanical elements outside.

LEFT & FAR LEFT
The studio balances creativity and quiet time with practical working elements such as expansive tables for overhead flat-lay photography. It also allows Harriet to enjoy positive connections with her favourite things. Flowers and treasured family hand-me-downs make this a very personal retreat.

Both to curb costs and because it was more in keeping with her values, Harriet rescued various other materials for the project. The flooring came from the dining room of a friend and was paid for with a slap-up lunch. Patched up in parts, the odd planks bring their own character to the space. One window came from a friend who was renovating her house and another from Facebook Marketplace. In the end, the only new elements were the corrugated tin roof and the tongue-and-groove interior cladding, which is made from FSC-certified pine. The decking and exterior walls are painted in Ronseal's Tudor Black Oak fence treatment.

OPPOSITE
The interior is spacious, with enough room for Harriet to work and move around, but it still retains a cosy quality. All the large items of furniture are freestanding so that the studio can be adapted for visiting groups, workshops and talks.

RIGHT
Harriet inherited this beautiful ottoman from her grandmother. It has a lovely shape, but the original upholstery was looking rather worn, so it has been re-covered in a classic monochrome floral fabric from Cabbages & Roses.

For the interior, Harriet made her own colour wash using a watered-down blend of Little Greene's Slaked Lime emulsion.

All the furnishings have been sourced over time, as Harriet waited for the right pieces to become available rather than rushing to kit out the space. Furniture was either brought from the main house or found in junk shops, at flea markets or online. Some items have a particular emotional resonance, such as an upholstered seat that had once belonged to Harriet's grandmother and still had years of use left in it.

RIGHT
An abundant supply of vases and other small vessels is essential for a botanical photographer. Harriet has opted for one-of-a-kind vintage designs in pressed and cut glass so that the full length of each flower is visible above and below the waterline. The submerged stem is just as precious as the bloom itself.

Now re-covered in Cabbages and Roses fabric, it stands by the window and serves as a reminder of past times and a favourite person. There are other sentimental finds, too, from Harriet's mother: steps from her kitchen, vases from around her home and veranda chairs from her garden.

Some of the fixtures and fittings play two roles in the studio, providing practical storage as well as decorative appeal. A huge cupboard that has belonged to Harriet for 25 years has been restored and repainted in Farrow & Ball's Off-Black in a dead flat finish. It now holds vases, linens and backgrounds that she uses for her photography. The steps, which provide a higher vantage point for flat-lays and overhead shots, also serve as makeshift shelves. There are other small shelving units on walls and tables, of the kind used by gardeners to display plants and specimen stems. This theatrical assembly allows Harriet to arrange, prepare and study the flowers she photographs and also accommodates her botanical collections.

The studio is suitable for year-round use with thorough insulation, electric lighting and even a stove, which is fuelled with locally felled wood. Not only is it perfectly suited to Harriet's routine, it has surpassed her expectations and offered up other opportunities as her photographic pastime has developed into a profession.

THIS PAGE & OPPOSITE BELOW LEFT
Storage and display often go hand in hand, and here, Harriet has consolidated handsome examples of both. A beautiful enclosed store cupboard is an especially hard-working piece with lots of surfaces and shelves for tools and accessories. Hiding these away behind closed doors allows the table to take centre stage. This is where items from Harriet's collection can be brought out or put away as the seasons change.

"All the furnishings have been sourced over time, as Harriet waited for the right pieces to become available rather than rushing to kit out the space."

She now hosts creative workshops in the space and also rents it out as a location for photoshoots.

Harriet's own photography is inspired by her love of flora and fauna, so it was clear from the outset that her studio would need a strong connection with the outdoors. The windows and doors are frequently left open and flowers from the garden are brought in and out. One of her favourite additions to the studio is the veranda. She describes it as a great spot to relax throughout the day, from breakfast in the early morning sun to a quiet evening drink. It is a protected place on the threshold of nature, where she can relish spiritual and soulful exchanges with the wild.

The studio belongs entirely to Harriet to use for herself, a place to express her creativity and engage with kindred spirits both online and in person at workshops and photoshoots. It has been slowly shaped and gradually fashioned over time with a curated mix of reclaimed pieces so that everything sits together comfortably and feels just right. As if imitating the natural shifting of the seasons, the studio fits the pace of Harriet's photographic progress as well as providing a bridge to better wellbeing. It is a room within nature where she can visualize and bring to life her own personal delights, joys and dreams.

THIS PAGE

Many of the items that Harriet needs for her work have a quiet beauty in their usefulness, so they are left out on display or arranged within easy reach. Containers of cut flowers, bundles of folded fabric and rows of baskets illustrate not only what she does but also what interests her. They deliver additional decorative detail in their own make-up, too. Smooth stoneware, rough wicker, crumpled linen and cool glass elevate simple backdrops to corners of curiosity.

OPPOSITE

Harriet has effortlessly combined a variety of different surface finishes in her studio. She has also demonstrated a creative use of paint in her inexpensive homemade colour wash for the tongue-and-groove walls. The recipe is based on Little Greene's Slaked Lime emulsion, which was watered down to allow knots and gnarls to show through. The translucent finish sits in considered contrast to the pristine new ceiling and the darker reclaimed flooring.

THIS PAGE

Jo and Tim's former railway carriage is now a static cabin – an inviting place to sit and relax comprising a sheltered outdoor space with facilities to cook, sleep and wash indoors. Taking a balanced, budget-friendly approach, the couple looked for reclaimed and vintage building materials. The result is a retreat that revives the comforts and novelties of the past, and is filled with travel-inspired details.

JOURNEY'S *end*

Inheriting a former railway wagon with the purchase of their Cambridgeshire property led Jo and Tim Ward to travel back down memory lane and add a personal touch to their holiday retreat.

Time had not been kind to the old wagon, which stood in a paddock on the edge of the farmland that surrounds Jo and Tim's family home. It had been there since the 1960s, when the local train line was decommissioned, and was used for many years as a shelter for orphan lambs. The wagon's decrepit state unfortunately meant that it would not be possible to renovate it, but the Wards could see the potential of its picturesque setting and sunset views. This gave them the idea of replacing it with a newly converted carriage as a wild retreat for guests to enjoy.

With the help of a local restoration company, the old wagon was lifted out and taken away. Jo and Tim then spent three months clearing the area, sowing wildflower seeds, preparing the services and laying railway sleepers/ railroad ties for the replacement carriage to sit on. They even built a new lamb shelter using reclaimed timber.

The 'new' wagon, supplied by the restoration company, is a similar vintage to the previous one: a 12-tonne/13-US-ton covered fruit wagon from the 1930s, still with its original barrel-vaulted roof timbers and oak flooring. Jo loves to imagine all the things it has carried and the places it has been over the years. With no concrete used in the installation process, the entire structure can be lifted away in the future and no one would know it had been there.

ABOVE
There are places to perch dotted around
the retreat for guests to discover, such
as this pair of swing chairs suspended
from the tree canopy. Shaded from the
elements, they offer a peaceful place to
kick back and relax away from it all.

The wagon's dark green exterior blends in beautifully with the tree canopy.
An additional veranda with matching green canvas offers additional shade and
shelter. Sustainability being of great importance, solar panels provide much
of the electricity, and the water for bathing comes from a borehole. Inside,
it is warm and snug thanks to a combination of eco-friendly wool insulation,
tongue-and-groove boards and a wood-burning stove. The interior represents
a creative collaboration between the reclaimed and the sustainably made.

Jo's family history has influenced the decoration just as much as the
wagon's own heritage. Her maternal grandfather William, who moved from
Wales to London as a young man, worked for Great Western Railway's catering
department. Jo was born in London, but she and her mother spent their
holidays in William's home town of Tenby in Pembrokeshire and they later
moved there when Jo was seven. As a result, she spent much of her youth
travelling by train with the perk of free rail travel thanks to William's job. The
comfort and charm of carriage life made an enduring mark on her and she has
furnished the wagon with an assortment of family-owned vintage pieces that
hark back to the period. The dark-wood furniture and vintage tablecloths of
her childhood appear alongside found and reclaimed pieces from secondhand
stores and jumble trails. Racks and overhead shelving made of reclaimed
timber resemble the original neat luggage racks, while a king-size storage bunk
from Ikea brings modern-day space-saving benefits to the sleeper-train setting.

Galley kitchen cabinets constructed out of timber offcuts are topped with a work surface made from old floorboards with a dark wax finish. A neat WC cubby is housed at the other end. Wall lights, handles and hinges throughout gleam with a traditional polished-brass finish.

Outdoors, visitors are encouraged to enjoy the peace and stillness, which is ironic considering the carriage's previous life. There is a rocking chair nearby and a dining table is sited just outside with a firepit for evening warmth. Up in the adjoining woods is an alfresco bathtub and shower. Beneath the walnut tree with its station signage, a pair of hanging chairs looks out over the field. In dappled sunlight it is the perfect spot for quiet contemplation.

The Wildflower Wagon's namesake blooms provide a steady season of change for pollinators and guests alike. With something new popping up each week, there is no need to venture far. The whole set-up looks back to the simpler times of Jo's childhood and encourages winding down. The many railway trinkets and treasures rekindle cherished memories, allowing guests to embark on a new quieter and calmer journey into the past.

ABOVE
A corner stove offers warmth and an additional cooking space in the form of a hotplate, which can heat kettles and pans. Locally felled wood is stored underneath.

RIGHT
The WC has been furnished with slimline fittings, including a compact reclaimed basin and a neat folding mirror, to offer the best washing facilities in a small space.

OPPOSITE
Snugness meets storage at the bunk end of the cabin. The bed is surrounded on three sides by panelling for a cocoon-like feel. The drawers underneath are a useful space in which to stow spare bedding and other essentials. Reclaimed linens have been ingeniously repurposed as curtains with the edges left raw. Their hanging threads and crumpled quality bring a carefree cosiness.

ON THE WATER

LEFT

The cabin's proximity to the
sea and the unrivalled coastal
scenery meant a deck area
was a must. A timber platform
was installed to raise the
deck up to the height of the
building and bring a wider
panorama into view. A canopy
offers dedicated shade and
protection from the elements.
Freestanding furniture allows
maximum flexibility. The
sofa arrangement seen here
is sometimes replaced with a
table and chairs for outdoor
dining or removed entirely
for larger gatherings.

SHORELINE *spirit*

With breathtaking views from its Cornish clifftop
position, interior designer Linda Dannvin's cabin
is the perfect coastal escape, but it's the cosy and
soulful details inside that make her retreat a real find.

With a setting surrounded by constantly changing sea and sky
views, the atmosphere and mood in the cabin frequently shift with
the weather and the tides. To balance this scene, she has created
a constant and considered setting inside her home-from-home
haven, which makes it feel spiritually connected to the coast yet
grounded and comfortable for day-to-day living.

When she first visited the property, which was then a tired
and run-down bungalow, Linda could see beyond the jaded decor
and overgrown garden, but it was the paddock in front that sealed
the deal. The sight of grazing horses and donkeys to welcome her
home from her frequent travels was the final tick on her wish list.

THIS PAGE
A sleek modern hob/stovetop has been fitted on a specially placed central island unit in the kitchen area to the rear of the cabin. It is almost completely flush to the worktop, and with the surfaces kept free of clutter, the streamlined setting allows for whoever is cooking to look up and out of the cabin. Practical pendants and a side window provide additional light in what could have been a gloomy space.

She knew that this bolthole base would become a place where she could rest, relax and regenerate between commitments.

Inspired by Linda's native Sweden and her many adventures abroad, the house has a holiday/vacation feeling. A happy cultural clash of beach, Scandi and chilled-out island vibes flows through her home. Aware that the bungalow's interior could easily resemble a box, Linda went about adding character with measured architectural details during the initial renovation phase.

RIGHT
Having a few freestanding items brings flexibility to a fitted kitchen and can help to break up the uniformity. Here, an antique wooden butcher's block and distressed wall unit have a charming vintage appeal and allow for impromptu use and display.

BELOW
Linda's 'homely minimal' kitchen unites clean lines with subtly softer details. These include the delicate blush tones of a raw plaster wall and the scuffed texture of an antique shelf board.

Unfinished elements are embraced, as were building materials that would normally be hidden away. Steel roof beams have been left exposed indoors and highlighted with blush-hued paint, while the ceilings and some walls have retained their raw plaster finish. Linda also introduced reclaimed elements such as worn timber and window shutters for an old-meets-new vibe.

Furniture and fittings mirror the salvaged building materials. Vintage and distressed elements bring a lived-in look to counter the formerly stark space. Peeled and puckered paintwork, gnarled woods and oxidized metal add a steadying, satisfying feel with their aged and authentic appearance.

A palette of warm, comforting hues was chosen to complement the raw materials and the natural landscape outside the windows.

RIGHT
Linda chose to bring together an assortment of lighting styles rather than a matching set. This allowed for easier room-zoning and it was a treat for Linda to track down so many different designs: sheer covered pendants, raffia and string wall lights and modern metal and acrylic shades and bases. This clever styling idea has resulted in shapely statement illumination.

"Peeled and puckered paintwork, gnarled woods and oxidized metal add a steadying, satisfying feel with their aged and authentic appearance."

LEFT

Linda has introduced seating areas in most of the rooms, some close to the windows and others in quiet corners. At times we all prefer to withdraw to a soulful and silent sanctuary. These inviting perches feature all kinds of seats, including antique chairs, wooden settles, padded pouffes and simple stools.

ABOVE

Although the cabin has the same floor plan as the original bungalow, Linda has added a few clever architectural details. In the bedroom, a shallow beam near one end forms a textural line to mark out the bathing zone. The walls have a semi-satin paint finish up to picture-rail height, then raw plaster above to match the ceiling. This textural contrast draws the eye upward.

RIGHT
Linda designed picture windows, and doors, to frame all the views. Crittall-style metal casements have been fitted with expansive panes of glass, some of which extend from floor to ceiling. Others are tailored to facilitate various interior activities. Next to the clawfoot bathtub, this useful window ledge is perfect for candles or drinking glasses. The window itself brings the amazing view inside as the light shines in and laps over the interior. The single-paned windows are a practical choice for coastal conditions and inclement weather, as they are much easier to clean than multiple smaller panes.

Blush shades from the plasterwork, a soft plum paint on the beams and coral-coloured linens sit with whitewashed layers, creating a harmonious, soothing scheme.

Textiles have been used to soften lines and surfaces. Filmy voiles draped at the windows provide shade, privacy and movement. Ruched linens and relaxed cushions/pillows are casually draped and scattered on the beds and sofa to give an air of ease, while rugs temper noise and add softness underfoot.

Cosy and intimate details have been installed to cater for easy modern living. The wood-burning stove has been raised off the floor to bring the fire in view when lit. A wall nook discreetly houses a television, which can be manoeuvred and angled so that the screen is visible from the bathtub in the bedroom. The tub itself features a handy distressed shelf alongside it, which is perfect for candles and drinks. The original bathroom was divided into two spaces that now house an ensuite shower room and connecting vanity to allow for unobtrusive dressing.

The expansive windows allow for daylight to flood into the rooms, but when it is darker there are copious candles and lamps. Allowing for a range of illumination, some lamps are covered with fabric shades, others in wire or wicker, the textures creating differing effects that can be dimmed or brightened at the flick of a switch.

The entire house has been designed to allow for an extraordinary exchange between the retreat and the coast. There is a mighty connection with nature where the sea and sky engage and entertain, but the backdrop also allows for the chance to lose oneself in watching the weather and the waves. The synergy between the setting and the scenery is unmistakable and Linda has created a haven for a holistic stay. It offers a cathartic experience, whether you are there for a fleeting visit or a longer spell.

THIS PAGE & OPPOSITE

Linda has opted for a pale colour palette throughout with earthy tones and textures. Raffia, wicker and straw mingle with woollens, felted cushions and seersucker linens. Inspired by the coastal setting, bed linens and drapery are layered to echo the ebb and flow of the water and sand. The look is unstructured and casual in tone. Equally uncomplicated are the loosely hung sheer drapes at the windows. These rarely need to be drawn for privacy, but instead offer unfussy shade from the sun.

NATURAL *tonic*

What was once an old birdwatching hide on the bank of an ancient horse pond is now a soulful sanctuary for Jo and Tim Ward and their guests at their B&B abode in Cambridgeshire.

BELOW & RIGHT
The lakeside setting is a fantastic area to engage with the great outdoors. A terraced seating area made of existing pavers has been created just outside the cabin. Beyond the terrace is a campfire surrounded by gravel, which is kept in place on one side by tree branches sourced from the grounds. On the other side, the gravel surface meets the pond's wildlife-friendly wetland and marginal planting.

Reimagining the crumbling structure and tackling the stagnant pond was not for the faint-hearted. However, Jo and Tim, whose Wildflower Wagon is featured on pages 74–79, could see the benefits of having a nature reserve on their doorstep and were keen to embrace the joys of being in and around the water.

Beginning with the pond, the couple sought online help from natural pool expert David Pagan Butler. Following his advice, they cleared vast amounts of sludge and replaced it with gravel and sand. They then installed an air pump system and added lots of native water plants for filtration. Within eight months, the transformation was complete. With no need for cleaning chemicals, the pond is now brimming with waterlilies, newts and dragonflies, and is visited by all kinds of birds. A soothing swim among all this wildlife is a natural antidote to fast-paced modern living.

The second stage of the project was initiated by the collapse of the pondside hide during the pandemic. As lockdown kicked in and shortages of materials and labour took hold, building a new structure became a team effort for Jo, Tim and their teenagers. It gave them a connection to nature during a stressful period and a place to escape for some alone time when 24/7 family life at the main house became too much.

LEFT
The outdoor area is hospitable for much of the year, thanks to the overhanging roofline. Plants offer additional natural screening and protection from the elements.

BELOW
If the weather does make it necessary to retreat inside the cabin, the interior is just as appealing as a place to dine or simply relax. Jo and Tim have furnished the space sustainably and inexpensively using a mix of secondhand and hand-me-down furniture and accessories.

OPPOSITE
The pond-facing wall of the cabin has expansive windows to take in the views. Clever planting allows guests to observe the wildlife unnoticed, a nod to the birdwatching hide that once stood here.

The new Dragonfly Cabin is a tin-roofed structure nestled between trees and the pool. Of great importance to the couple was that the construction be done as sustainably as possible. The cabin rests on 'feet', rather than on a solid platform, to keep the use of concrete to a minimum, and the exterior is clad in locally sourced larch. Good insulation keeps it cool in the summer and warm in the winter – it is the perfect spot in which to savour the location all year round. Outdoor living is very much encouraged, while the indoor space is an appealing place to shelter from inclement weather and a covered veranda bridges the threshold between the two. Doors can be left open at all hours, even at night, when there are various nocturnal sounds to enjoy.

Jo paid particular attention to potential views from the cabin and even lay down on the dusty floor during the build to ensure that the bed would have the perfect pool vista. This view is now a firm favourite thanks to a huge picture window, which offers an expansive panorama of the natural elements from a place of safety.

This is an architectural principle known as 'prospect-refuge' – a similar technique was used by the American designer Frank Lloyd Wright, who was particularly well known for his organic architecture. Here, the water reflects light into the cabin as well as bringing in all the soothing sounds and colours of nature. No matter what the time or season, the water creates magical reflections across the whitewashed ceiling.

The design of the cabin's interior was very much inspired by its setting and potential use. The small size meant it would need to be uncluttered but have everything guests might need to unwind within easy reach. A mostly monochrome colour palette with plenty of wood and other natural materials lends a Scandi feel. Oak floorboards in the bedroom, kitchen and living area give way to pebble flooring from Marble Mosaics in the bathroom. The shower is lined with copper, which has innate antibacterial properties and will develop a beautiful patina as it ages.

All the furniture is preloved or made from salvaged materials. The kitchen has been built using timber offcuts and topped with a reclaimed oak work surface, and there is also an old oak gateleg table that has been stripped and treated with lime wax. The stools and benches were created by a local carpenter Idea Tree Designs using scaffolding boards and left in their raw state to age. Characterful textiles include curtains made from Tinsmiths fabric and bed linen from Loaf. Plants, foraged finds and artwork depicting local flora all help to bring the tranquillity of the natural world inside.

The idea to renovate the pond and create this waterside retreat was initially devised for the benefit of guests, but in reality it has become something of a salvation for all the family to enjoy. It is a place where they can swim outdoors whatever the season, absorb the benefits of being in nature and experience a habitual and harmonious exchange with the wild.

THIS PAGE
According to Jo, the bed offers the best views in the cabin. It is also the most comfortable place to experience the goings-on around the pond and pier. Guests can rest here while watching the wildlife during the day and go to sleep at night listening to the soothing sounds of the pond's nocturnal visitors.

OPPOSITE
Choosing a layout is a major decision when renovating a canal boat. You can run galley rooms from one end to the other or zone off one or both ends to create self-contained spaces. Sam went with the latter approach. Adapting the side door to make it the main entrance has enabled her to establish a permanent living area at one end, complete with a fitted sofa bed.

RIGHT & BELOW
Despite its urban setting in central London, *Velvet Morning* has a peaceful and calm mooring in a tree-lined canal basin. Should Sam want a change of scene, she can easily take the boat on a trip out to a new stretch of water.

NARROW *escape*

It was the desire to shift down a gear that led Sam Barbic to begin her renovation of *Velvet Morning*, a traditional narrowboat that has become a beautiful canalside sanctuary in the heart of London.

Modern living often goes at such a great pace that sometimes it is important to step back and put the brakes on. Such was the case for the stylist and set designer Sam Barbic. After being diagnosed with cancer, she had had a long spell of being unwell and dealing with the stresses of treatment. Sam found she wanted, or rather needed, a place where she could wind down, disconnect and do something entirely different from her busy day-to-day life. The freedom of the canal-boat lifestyle struck a chord.

In a narrowboat it is essential to make the most of the space, which can lead to some unique solutions. A window in the kitchen has been styled with practicality in mind – herbs in pots thrive on the sill and a humble blind/shade is held in place with pegs/clothespins (right). Beside the cooker/stove, a small work surface holds condiments and tableware (far right).

Designing Airbnbs for a friend was proof that Sam had a gift for styling small spaces, and she had fond memories of attending her aunt's wedding on a canal boat as a child. More recently, she visited a good friend who had sold up to live on one. On hand near Sam's home in London, the waterways of the local canal basin offered a new view on life, whether moored up or on the move. After weeks of looking at boats for sale, Sam happened upon *Velvet Morning*, whose name was *Fern* back then. She drove to Bath for a viewing and soon realized that this was the one.

A simple refurb soon turned into a major job with a steep learning curve. However, the reclamation and revamp of the 100-year-old craft proved to be a therapeutic experience, too.

LEFT & OPPOSITE

The galley-style kitchen and dining area occupies the centre of the boat. The kitchen is very well equipped with plenty of storage in the form of cabinets and shelving. Next to the dining table on the opposite wall, a wood-burning stove provides warmth and also heats water for the radiators. Doorways lead through to the bathroom and bedroom at the rear, which can be closed off for privacy when required.

It was originally a 'butty boat', a cargo narrowboat that has no engine and has to be towed along. Although an engine had since been installed, there was a need for remodelling inside and out. The boat had been on a permanent mooring in a marina, so everything needed rewiring to run on batteries, which are charged by solar panels on the roof. New windows had to be custom made because of their unusual shapes and sizes. Finally, the exterior was stripped back and repainted and a new name was found. *Velvet Morning* comes from the title of a song by Lee Hazlewood and Nancy Sinatra, which is a favourite of Sam's.

Inside, the original oak flooring had rotted due to a leak. A new subfloor was laid in the bathroom, then all the floorboards were sanded back and finished with a natural oil made by Osmo. In order to lighten up the internal space, all the interior wood panelling was painted in various off-white shades from Farrow & Ball, including All White in the main living area and the softer Cornforth White in the bedroom.

The new interior is divided into four zones: from the living room in the bow, oak panelled doors lead through to the kitchen, then the bathroom and finally the bedroom at the stern. With the help of a local carpenter, bespoke cupboards have been fitted into odd angles and under seating and beds. Kitchen cabinets have slotted neatly into place with extra shelving above. An antique reclaimed Belfast sink was fitted here and a waney-edge piece of oak from a reclamation yard has been repurposed as a work surface. All the unpainted wooden surfaces have been finished with Osmo oil, which brings out the warmth and texture of the natural grain.

OPPOSITE & ABOVE
An impressive bathroom has been installed within the narrow space. A freestanding clawfoot tub like this one will generally take up less floor space than a built-in design because there is no need for a boxy bath panel. A mirrored vanity seems to disappear against the wall, but provides lots of storage space behind its closed doors. The window above the basin brings the canalside birdlife up close.

"The interior decoration is shaped by simple cabin comforts in a harmonious palette of neutrals and natural touches, with a few hints of luxury."

LEFT & BELOW LEFT
Wall space in the bedroom is utilized for storage as well as sleeping. The child-size built-in bunk has space underneath for large items, including anything that doesn't fit into the smaller cupboards and compartments on board. A wall-mounted shelf to one side allows treasured belongings to be seen but kept out of the way.

RIGHT
The platform-style double bed is located in the stern of the boat, in front of the original access door, which now acts as a kind of headboard. There is a narrow shelf all around the bed, which is used for decorative display as well as somewhere to place a water glass. Sam has fitted curtain rods above and below the windows. As a result, the curtains follow the angle of the sloping walls rather than hanging straight down and leaving gaps.

The interior decoration is shaped by simple cabin comforts in a harmonious palette of neutrals and natural touches, with a few hints of luxury such as a full-size bed and comfortable seating. The blinds/shades and curtains were all made from organic linens and Indian block prints from The Cloth Shop on Portobello Road in London. Personal touches come in the form of considered and carefully chosen vintage belongings: artwork made from pressed flowers found on the canal, antique brass hooks and hangers from reclamation yards and pewter vases sourced from markets. The antique pulley-style clothes airer that hangs above the bathtub is both practical and beautiful. Avoiding nautical clichés, each of these everyday items is handsome in its own simple way.

The boat exists completely off-grid thanks to the solar panels, which usually generate enough power for all the lights and electrical appliances. If additional energy is required, this can be achieved by running the engine for just an hour a day. To make sure the interior would be warm and welcoming whatever the weather, Sam installed a reconditioned Morsø Squirrel multi-fuel stove and back boiler to provide hot water and heat the radiators.

The finished result is an inviting and uplifting haven from everyday life. Even though *Velvet Morning* is moored in central London, it has been designed to offer a gentler pace and a sense of balance. Life on the water has given Sam a chance to experience the changing seasons, from relaxing on deck in the summer to warming up by the fire in the winter. A wonderful added bonus has been getting to know the canalside community. Sam has since acquired a second barge (see pages 106–113) and now offers them as places to rent out so that others can enjoy the calming virtues of canal life. On board *Velvet Morning*, there is no rush to motor along on the water, only carefree cruising.

BROAD *horizons*

After catching the boating bug with *Velvet Morning* (see pages 98–105), Sam Barbic acquired a second barge named *Wide Beam*, which she has reimagined as a Japandi-style floating hideaway in London's Little Venice.

Sam had narrowly missed out on the chance to purchase *Wide Beam* once before, so when it came back on the market just 12 months later, she felt that this time it was meant to be. Fortunately, the seven-year-old boat was already solid and watertight with a good layout. At 16.8 x 3 metres/55 x 10ft, it also feels much more spacious inside than a typical 2.1-metre/7ft-wide narrowboat. It was just the design and finish that needed a bit of TLC, which stylist Sam was naturally able to provide.

ABOVE & OPPOSITE
The viewing platform at the bow has been planted to become a wonderful balcony just off the bedroom (above). On the spacious roof deck above, freestanding pots add to the abundance of greenery (opposite). There is space to sunbathe and even a fire pit. When not in use, this large flat area is handy for storage.

LEFT
Sam has chosen to run a continuous hallway along the full length of the boat. From the garden balcony at the front, French windows lead down into the main bedroom. The glazing allows light into the space, while the voile curtain can be pulled across when privacy is needed.

ABOVE

The bedroom features a
bespoke platform bed with
open shelving built into
one side of the headboard
and cupboards underneath.
The headboard itself has
been carefully shaped to
fit the angles and curves of
the barges's interior. It has
integrated electrical sockets/
outlets for lamps and chargers
and an alcove space for
personal items. The plywood
shelf matches the panelling
on the walls and ceiling.

Below deck, the cavernous main living space comprises a kitchen, seating area a
nd office/snug. Even with an open-plan layout, space-saving solutions are the key to
any successful boat design, so every nook has been put to use. There is plentiful storage
in the kitchen and handcrafted cupboards under the bed. The hallway houses a run
of shelving, with a wet room hidden behind and a bedroom in the bow. The cabin-like
interior has an easy flow, which is complemented by its minimal, East-meets-West decor.

Sam drew inspiration for the project from places she has visited on her travels and
especially from the clean lines and simplicity of Japanese and Scandinavian design.
The result is a modern interior that unites a striking mix of cultural references. Natural
materials provide gentle colour and texture. The plywood cladding on the walls and
ceilings is made from birch, which is a fast-growing species and thus a sustainable choice.
Neat gaps between the panels are a sign of modest craftsmanship. A host of houseplants
brings the outside world inside. The overall effect is organic and feels very different to
the dark, varnished wood of a traditional narrowboat interior.

RIGHT

The hallway houses multipurpose storage along the length of the boat. Sam has cleverly hidden away a wet room just off this area – the entrance is stepped back from the deep shelves.

BELOW RIGHT

Sam combined the previously separate shower and WC to create the new wet room. Removing the wall has allowed for a much better use of space, with a shower curtain as a temporary partition. Bathroom basics are kept dry in sealed cabinets.

BELOW

The vanity and wall cabinet were chosen for their clean lines and shipshape qualities, and also for their finishes. Metallic and mirrored surfaces maximize the amount of light, which compensates for the small size of the porthole window.

"Sam drew inspiration from places she has visited on her travels, especially from the clean lines and simplicity of Japanese and Scandinavian design."

For contrast, monochromatic colour appears in the form of painted surfaces, stitched textiles and more. The feature wall behind the stove is lined with encaustic Alalpardo tiles by Bert & May, while the bathroom is tiled with a smaller-scale penny mosaic design. Fabricated stainless steel on the kitchen walls is a practical and low-maintenance option that helps to define this area within the larger open-plan space.

Sam has finished the interior with shapely freestanding furniture, which offers maximum flexibility. The stylish Habitat sofa, which folds out into a snug bed, was chosen as much for its versatility and boat-friendly size as for its soft green upholstery. A bench, also from Habitat, can be easily packed away and the desk and chair moved around as needed. If additional sleeping accommodation is required, there are futon-style mattresses made from Indian block-printed cotton, which are rolled up when not in use. These are also useful for sunbathing on the roof deck in warm weather.

Wicker basketry and simple cushions/pillows in jute, wool and cotton were sourced from two Danish brands, Madam Stoltz and Bloomingville, which supply homewares made by Indian craftspeople. Both companies nurture traditional skills and support the economy of rural villages, which is very important to Sam.

LEFT & RIGHT
The living space has been cleverly carved up with different floor heights. The main area is at the lowest point of the boat. Partly hidden by the feature wall Sam installed behind the stove is a study space that can also be used for sleeping (left). Freestanding furniture makes the space very adaptable, as items can be moved to wherever they are needed (right).

RIGHT
Part of the shelving rack along the corridor is open on both sides. This means that Sam's decorative displays can be seen and admired from both the corridor and the study. It also allows for natural light to pass through from one side of the boat to the other.

Japanese references can be seen in the embroidery stitching on favourite cushions/ pillows and in the repurposed hemmed linen that has been crafted into simple cabin-style curtains and drapes. In the bedroom, buff, nude and plaster-pink linens from Toast c onvey a sensuous, nurturing mood.

The natural environment is very much part of the experience of being on board. The boat sits low in the water, so the light reflecting off the rippling waves casts shimmering highlights and silhouettes on the walls and ceilings. Birds and wildlife beckon at the doors and windows, including a side hatch that offers wonderful views of the sky in all kinds of weather. Upstairs, there is the roof deck with its own firepit.

And then there is a watery world on the doorstep just waiting to be explored – Sam's favourite places in London to travel by boat are Camden, King's Cross and Shoreditch. Her travel-inspired barge is always ready to pack up with ease and set out on its next voyage.

ABOVE
The walls in the kitchen are lined with stainless steel. Frequently found in commercial catering settings, it is a very practical and low-maintenance surface that is easy to keep clean. It also reflects light and brings a contemporary touch to the decor.

RIGHT
Even though the barge's interior is primarily modern, Sam has included charming touches that tie into nature and bring life to the

otherwise minimal scheme. She loves to incorporate plants and cut flowers, which complement the natural materials and organically shaped homewares.

OPPOSITE
Sam opted to clad the walls and ceilings throughout with boards made of birch wood. Sustainable, malleable and easy to cut, the timber offered many benefits as well as being cost-effective. The boards were left in their natural finish, which has a subtle warmth.

SOULFUL *service*

Formerly the home of a military officer's batman, Miranda Gardiner's riverside cabin in Devon is an atmospheric, calming and considered place that stands at ease in its surroundings and holds lingering memories of bygone days.

With the River Avon on its doorstep and the coast not far away, this heritage summerhouse naturally houses a few shoreline finds, but it is the nod to its unique history that makes the cabin stand out from the crowd. It was built in the 1930s as an orderly home for the manservant, or batman, of a military gentleman who lived nearby. The building was constructed from local timber, with windows overlooking the river. It came complete with an attached greenhouse and its own garden, all sited within the boundary of the property where Miranda lives with her husband Diggory.

ABOVE LEFT & LEFT
The retreat is sited on an elevated bank of the River Avon (above left). Its large windows frame views of the rippling waters (left). The picturesque setting attracts all kinds of wildlife: songbirds, winged insects, fish and river-dwelling mammals. Nature watching and listening are the most pleasurable of pastimes in this peaceful pocket of countryside.

OPPOSITE
The cabin has a practical layout that makes the best use of the space. The central living room has various entryways that open off it. One of these is a glass door leading to the main bedroom at ground level. There is just enough roof space for a small second room above under the rafters. This is reached via a stair ladder, which has been cleverly tucked away behind the chimney breast so as not to interrupt the flow of the living space below.

Despite its age, the cabin's original structure turned out to be sound, with only the windows, the flooring and the rickety greenhouse needing to be replaced. Miranda and Diggory's first priority was a rethink of the layout. There are now two bedrooms (one on a mezzanine level) and a bathroom at one end of the cabin, where the kitchen used to be, and an open-plan living area and galley kitchen at the other. The tongue-and-groove panelling in the new kitchen was taken from the original kitchen, and the wide floorboards throughout are made from larch wood that the couple harvested in the Avon Valley 10 years ago. They finished the boards using Sikkens's oil-based wood stain in Ebony. On the site of the old greenhouse there is now a dining area with sliding screen windows made by carpenter Jeremy Wright of Churchstow. New oak flooring resembles a boat deck and makes the interior feel shipshape.

The cabin's pale, understated colour palette includes grey and khaki shades, which tie into its military origins. Against this simple backdrop, dark-coloured hardwood furniture and fittings look back to how the interior might have been furnished in the 1930s and 1940s. The kitchen cabinetry was made from reclaimed cupboards and finished in the same dark wood stain that was used on the flooring. The mahogany-coloured sapele-wood work surfaces were painted with food-safe tung oil.

Polished-brass details in the kitchen and beyond gleam brightly like uniform buttons, including vintage handles found at Totnes market, lighting, taps/faucets, hooks and rails. Of particular note is the splashback behind the cooker/stove, which was ingeniously formed from a brass coal bucket that has been unfurled and hammered flat. Behind the kitchen sink, a slab of antique marble from Two Rooms in Kingsbridge has been mounted on the wall. These make-do-and-mend details hark back to the origins of the building, as do the Gardiners' collections of antique pots and pans. Favourites include a brass tea strainer and colander that have been in the family for generations. The look is a perfect combination of function and form.

Much of the furniture has been nimbly handcrafted and several pieces have been made bespoke to fit the cabin's proportions – a technique often found in boat interiors. The bathroom houses a unique washstand made by Diggory. A cupboard in the living room has been reworked and cut down in size. The twin beds upstairs have fetching headboards in book-matched mahogany, which were made by Staples & Co., a company founded in 1895. They once belonged to Miranda's mother's Auntie Ruth, who ran a B&B in Cornwall, and were later used by the Gardiners' children before finding a home here.

Practical but elegant textiles are another common thread. Beds are made up with simple linens, and understated curtains frame the garden and river views. Upholstery that might have had a much more prim and proper fit back in the 1930s is today relaxed and inviting.

OPPOSITE & ABOVE

The kitchen has been repositioned within the cabin and rebuilt to make it more compatible with modern living (opposite). However, it retains a few elements of its previous incarnation, such as the tongue-and-groove panelling (above). The cabinets have been reworked to be a better fit with today's kitchenware and their surfaces freshened up with paint or varnish. The gold-leaf painting in the corner is the work of local artist Amanda Brooks.

RIGHT

A dining area has been established on the site of an old lean-to greenhouse. The curtains have eyelet headings, which require less fabric than pleats and have a more modern look. A rare-breed sheepskin from Søren Designs adds a touch of softness.

"The cabin's pale, understated colour palette includes grey and khaki shades, which tie into its military origins."

This easy-going approach is much better suited to modern times, in which fabrics can be allowed to crumple and crease for a more lived-in look. Modern practicalities also had an influence on the design of the bathroom, which has a tiled wet-room shower area with glazed doors rather than a traditional bathtub. The tiles add an unexpected block of pattern.

There is a selection of collected and considered personal pieces throughout, including genteel vintage photographs, original artworks and small decorative items. The works of art mostly belong to Miranda, who formerly worked as a curator, as do the European and British ceramics gathered over the past 20 years. There are subtle nautical elements, too, such as floats, basket nets and rope from Two Rooms. Softening the setting are indoor plants displayed from hanging boxes and vintage plant stands. The daily care and attention they require is a much-loved hobby for Miranda and not a chore.

Allowing easier access to the outside, the large windows open up and connect the interior with the garden, the deck and the river beyond. Wind-down time is encouraged by the close proximity of the calm of the water's edge. From the deck you can fish for wild salmon and trout, follow dragonflies as they dip in the water or simply watch the river as it ripples past. The cabin radiates the life of a slower but satisfying era, a rhythm unchanged by the passing of many decades. A feeling of unhurried leisure comes from a space that harmoniously melds the past with the present, where one can enjoy timeless tasks in an understated yet inviting environment.

OPPOSITE
One of Miranda's favourite areas is the upstairs bedroom, which shares her own history as well as that of its former owner. The two twin beds, which are shown here combined into a double, have headboards that have been used by multiple generations of her relatives. They have now found a new home here at the cabin. It's a wonderful full-circle story of keeping things in the family and finding uses for them as life and situations change.

ABOVE
The bathroom has been designed for maximum functionality. It is divided into thirds, with a wet-room area at one end, a basin in the middle and a WC near the door. In a small room, spatial planning is key – you need to consider what can be walked past, what requires space to use and what needs to be contained. Diggory adapted the charming wooden vanity to fit within the compact layout and now it proudly takes centre stage.

LEFT

The cabin has been beautifully crafted by Matt, who is a carpenter by trade. The feather-edged Douglas fir boards used for the cladding on the lower level are a simple yet weatherproof option, as they allow rain to drip down and keep the joints hidden. Above, Matt has created a more decorative finish with a painstaking arrangement of log ends. Wonderfully pleasing to the eye, it also provides a habitat for insects to enjoy.

BELOW LEFT

The entrance area combines homely touches with tempting views. The open-plan design enables the panorama to be seen from everywhere once inside. The wavy pendant lampshade is from a collaboration by Munro and Kerr and A Considered Space.

RIGHT

The whole of the rear wall has been fitted with floor-to-ceiling glazed doors, which can be slid back to create an even more seamless transition to the balcony beyond. When the doors are closed, an eco-friendly ethanol stove keeps the cabin cosy and inviting, even on cold days.

WILD *wonder*

Taking the slow, considered approach to design and decor, Harriet Churchward and Matt Pescod have shaped the style and spirit of their amazing treehouse in Herefordshire. Their creative vision has come to life in this truly enchanting woodland retreat.

The siting of the cabin on a slope means that the balcony is much further from the ground than the front entrance. Tree trunks thread through the elevated platform, which feels like part of the forest canopy. This design detail allows for direct engagement with the woodland and its inhabitants. The balcony table is dressed with a hand-printed tablecloth from The Campbell Collection.

The treehouse was always intended as a place where the couple and their guests could escape for short breaks and longer stays. Harriet and Matt found their inspiration in American cabins of old with their simple and functional yet homely styling. These hardy dwellings were built to withstand all weathers and look better with age, and the couple were drawn to their practical and personal design details. They imagined guests coming and going freely in heavy boots and coats, and hunkering down in the comfiest and most welcoming of cabins. Born from this small acorn of an idea, the treehouse now stands in the grounds of Brinsop Court, a 14th-century manor owned by Harriet's parents. It is the result of a thoughtful design and building process thst spanned a period of three years.

As a carpenter-builder by trade, Matt contributed his skills and experience to the project, with help from architect Will Millward. Choosing to work with wood seemed an obvious decision for a woodland cabin, and the couple were keen to use sustainable and recycled materials throughout. The frame and cladding are made of Douglas fir, the floorboards are oak and the gable end of the structure has been finished with log ends hewn from the estate and placed by hand. The whole thing is sited on a concrete-free foundation system that has been piled into the ground. The cabin now cuts a handsome figure in the woods. Inside, artisan building techniques and details bring additional textures and surface finishes. A thatched ceiling can be found in one of the bedrooms and raw plaster walls in the bathroom. Oak offcuts have been repurposed as panelling for the bathroom ceiling.

Harriet and Matt researched the safest and most stylish way to heat and light a wooden home all year round that would also be in keeping with the interior. A chimney-free ethanol stove was chosen as a clean-burning and easy-to-use solution. Lighting has been used to create zones and cosy corners in the open-plan layout – the house had to be candle free, so the couple have used carefully placed lamps and pendants to establish the right ambience in each space. Sauna lights were reimagined as task lamps in the kitchen, which also has a pendant to cast a wider glow. Instead of running cables into the middle of the open-plan space to illuminate the main seating area, the pair dropped pendants over the sofa arms and placed extra lamps around the perimeter as required. The dining area has a beautiful overhead light that adds atmospheric focus during mealtimes and, if lowered, emulates candlelight.

ABOVE RIGHT & RIGHT
An outdoor hot tub (above right) and shower (right) bring the opportunity to bathe in and under water in the wild. The tub is warmed by a wood fire and the shower plumbed in from the main bathroom, so they both offer hot temperatures even on the coldest of days. The warmth allows for leisurely soaks and the chance for guests to enjoy a sensory exchange with the scenery as they bask under the open sky.

The furniture and fixtures throughout the treehouse have soft and comfortable shapes. Here, a family-size sofa faces the balcony. The chequered cushion/pillow on the armchair is from Eldorado The Studio. In the dining area, a banquette in the window is another inviting seat.

The cabin features a snug colour palette inspired by its wooden interior and echoing the forest setting. Harriet and Matt put together a mood board as a visual aid for the decoration. Mellow and easy-going shades of nut brown, mustard and terracotta sit with chalky whites, blues and greys on simple, stylish furniture. Antiques and art bring character and textiles have a softening effect. The kitchen cabinets sport cottage-style checked curtains and the dining table is dressed with primitive printed linens.

Upstairs, tent-like curtains screen and shade one of the two bedrooms, both of which have bespoke upholstered headboards, exquisite linens and tailor-made quilts.

To keep the living space looking streamlined, a sliding barn door has been fitted as an entrance to the bathroom. Neatly skimming the wall to the side, the d oor also complements the cabin setting with its simple design and wooden texture.

OPPOSITE & ABOVE
In the kitchen, nutmeg and terracotta shades add a prairie feel. The tiles on the work surface are from Topps Tiles and the under-counter curtains were made with fabric from Tinsmiths, while the brass Mayan taps/ faucets and hanging rail were sourced from DeVol. A wall-mounted metal plate rack from Stovold & Pogue in a smart Anthracite finish creates a slick storage feature.

The tented bedroom was designed in collaboration with the interior designer Sophie Rowell of Côte de Folk. She came up with the initial concept and gave guidance on the composition of the drapes, blinds/ shades and velvet headboard, while Harriet took care of the project management and sourced other elements such as the bed linen and cushions/pillows. The finished look is modern yet homespun.

The treehouse offers a unique woodland experience. Its large windows and balcony deck allow guests to observe the local wildlife. Around 100 bat boxes have been installed up in the forest canopy as well as houses for dormice low to the ground and salt licks for visiting deer. The cabin's log-end cladding even serves as a bug house. A wood-fired hot tub and shower bring guests closer to nature, and there is ample outdoor space for seating and dining.

Harriet and Matt's careful planning at every step of the way, from the initial blueprints to the finishing touches, has ensured that this retreat is well worth the wait. They have constructed a remarkable treehouse for kindred spirits to enjoy. It is a curated and soulful setting that welcomes with ease and leaves an enduring memory in the minds and hearts of all who enter.

ABOVE
The bathroom's luxurious freestanding tub from Lusso Stone is partitioned off by floor-to-ceiling curtains, which are gathered and tied back with rope loops. It is a simple idea, but the plentiful fabric gives the drapes a lavish look.

ABOVE RIGHT
A double vanity basin unit allows for shared and conversational washing. It also incorporates ample storage underneath. The under-counter curtain is a neat cover-up that hides clutter from view.

RIGHT
Romantically draped curtains can be found in the loft bedroom area, too, which was decorated with the help of interior designer Sophie Rowell. They screen off the bed from the large windows that look out over the balcony and beyond.

OPPOSITE
The front bedroom offers incredible natural textures, including a woven ceiling and sustainably sourced pinoleum blinds/shades. Bed linen by Society of Wanderers and Hunant adds colour and pattern.

LEFT & BELOW
The retreat is positioned directly under pinewood trees and is backed by the forest, which provides shelter from the weather (left). The simple yet modern structure has a sunny location at the top of a hill, so the interior is flooded with copious natural light throughout the day (below).

OPPOSITE
Dark, rich hues on internal walls and ceilings bring a touch of bold sophistication. The paint colour seen here is Studio Green by Farrow & Ball, a subtle green-black that echoes the wild woodland setting and harmonizes well with the dark timber cabinetry and warm metallic accents.

HIDE & *seek*

Keen to share the delights of the wilds and woods with others, James Roupell established Rest + Wild – a collective of mindful retreats designed to promote the restorative qualities of being outdoors. This cabin in Shropshire ticks all the boxes.

Hidden in one of the UK's Areas of Outstanding Natural Beauty, close to the border between England and Wales, Rest + Wild's Shropshire Hills Hideaway boasts breathtaking countryside views. It is located on the Downton Hall Estate, which extends to over 5,000 acres, comprising farmland, woodland and part of Titterstone Clee Hill. Full of warmth and character, The Sparrow is one of four cabins, each designed to feel like a home in nature. It is a refined, cosy space that reflects the distinctiveness of the surrounding countryside.

Inside, the decor is simple yet luxurious, with plenty of natural and reclaimed materials. The windows are kept fuss-free and are dressed with simple custom-made blinds/shades to make the most of the expansive views.

BELOW

The cabin is divided into a sleep and studio area with a bathroom to the rear accessed via a space-saving sliding door. A dark wooden screen separates the two spaces physically, but also links them aesthetically, as the same material was used for the kitchen cabinets and bathroom vanity. Open shelving, rails and hooks house useful kitchenalia, and gleaming metal pendants add a handsome finishing touch.

A dark palette echoes the feeling of being outside under the tree canopy, but also brings a handsome and smart style to the interior. Studio Green, a deep green paint from Farrow & Ball, is a bold yet comfortable choice – far from being dull and gloomy, the colour reflects the profusion of light coming in through the windows.

Furniture is a mix of built-in and fold-down to offer the best use of space and flexibility for easy living all year round. A small kitchen and bathroom feature toward the rear, with a bed at the window end to allow for lazing and lingering over the fantastic views. If the weather wanes, guests can cook and dine inside or sit on a locally sourced easy chair by the log-burning stove.

OPPOSITE

At the other end of the cabin, a platform bed has been fitted to enjoy panoramic views from picture windows on two sides, which bring the dramatic hillside and valley scenery right inside. Every effort has been made to ensure that the bed is inviting and comfortable. With the softest of linens and a wood-burning stove for warmth, it is the best place to relax, unwind and watch the wild world go by.

Even the smallest decorative details contribute to the humble-luxe feel. Soft, crumpled linen from Piglet in Bed promises a restful sleep, and the ceramic tableware is handmade by community members at a Camphill Village Trust for disabled adults. Kitchen accessories have been sourced from ethical homeware brand Nkuku, along with the elegant brass bedside lamps with their etched-glass shades. A rainfall shower in the bathroom offers a gentler cleanse and there are natural toiletries for guests to enjoy.

But it's outside where the chance to be at one with nature comes alive. Thankfully, everything you might need in order to live out under the sky and stars can be found here. This cabin represents the freedom to explore and a chance to discover all the joys of outdoor living. A deep and luxurious copper bathtub sits on a platform so that you can contentedly doze or gaze as you spa and soak. A firepit and griddle offer the chance for camp cookouts. After all, doesn't everything taste better outdoors?

James and his team have created a cosy and comfy cabin experience combining shelter and solace with easy-living extras in a private and perfect panorama. Each retreat is designed to be immersive and undisturbed, a soulful place in which to savour a slower pace and reap the benefits of spending time in nature.

OPPOSITE & RIGHT
The immediate outdoors brings the opportunity to bathe, dine and lounge outside while enjoying views of wild woodlands and tended pastures. A deep plunge bathtub offers piping-hot water for an indulgent forest spa experience (opposite). A campfire surrounded by comfortable seating is an inviting spot to cosy up in the evenings (right).

RIGHT
The cabin looks out over open fields, which are grazed by the estate farm's sheep. The animals themselves are also a pleasing sight for guests staying here. Observing the slow cycle of the farming year as it follows the seasons can help us feel a deeper connection to nature.

"*Intensive farming methods had taken their toll, eradicating the native plants and wildlife, so part of the new plan was to rewild the site.*"

LEFT

Sleeping, dining and cooking areas can be found both inside and outside the cabins. Weatherproof and practical outdoor furniture includes roughly hewn log stools as well as simple and stackable designs that can easily be styled up or stripped back.

RIGHT

A comprehensive fitted kitchen is raised up on a deck and sheltered from the elements by an overhead canopy, but still open to the fresh air. It is connected to the gas and electricity supply, and water is plumbed in from an isolated tank that can be refreshed when empty.

CALL OF *the wild*

After taking on a tumbledown Welsh cottage and a wayward farming wilderness, Jessie Roberts-Duffey and Lyndon Duffey have created a hidden escape for themselves and their loved ones. It is a unique place where they can embrace the rhythm of the seasons.

Beckoned back by memories of the community and countryside of their own Ceredigion childhoods, Jessie and Lyndon left their comfortable city lives for the chance to experience a more gratifying and grounded lifestyle. With a commitment to putting down rural roots, their aim was to create a restful, idyllic oasis for family and friends to enjoy and appreciate nature's own playground and pastimes.

THIS PAGE
This corner fitted sofa was built by Lyndon. One side has under-seat storage for luggage, while the other has a pull-out trundle bed underneath to transform it into an extra bunk. Simply furnished with mattresses and cushions/pillows, it is a comfy spot for carefree lounging.

ABOVE

The walls of the covered outdoor kitchen are a clever combination of solid metal and clear plastic sheeting, which lets in the daylight.

RIGHT

Inside, Lyndon has lined the walls with plenty of insulation, over which wooden boards have been fitted. The cabin is warm and inviting even in the coldest months, and the wood texture is both tactile and visually appealing.

Starting with a run-down smallholding complete with ramshackle pigsties and pens, Jessie and Lyndon have invested time and energy in rescuing the land. They wanted to make a place where they could reconnect and peacefully coexist with nature. The now wonderfully wild nature reserve at One Cat Farm is a vision of pastures and backwoods. A small collection of rustic cabins is dotted around absorbing ponds and field life.

At the beginning of this new journey, the couple and their children moved into the main cottage. However, it was the terrain that called to them first, such was its desperate state with outbuildings, tools and agricultural trappings strewn everywhere. Intensive farming methods had taken their toll, eradicating the native plants and wildlife, so part of the new plan was to rewild the site. Waste was removed, saplings were planted and, slowly but surely, the flora and fauna began to return in swathes, flocks and families.

PAGE 144

The bedroom area has been designed to make the most of the vista from the large picture window, with the bed built on a platform to ensure the best viewing position. There is an expansive storage space under the bed, and the top of the bespoke headboard doubles as a shelf for books and foraged finds.

To continue this sustainable exchange, Jessie and Lyndon initiated a prolonged plan for how to incorporate care and support for the environment from the ground up. The cabins were built from scratch using carbon-neutral wooden planks and beams, including larch for the external cladding, and with the aid of self-taught skills and a lot of patience. Tailor-made for the terrain, the retreats are warm and cosy all year round, burning locally sourced woods in the outdoor firepits. Plans are afoot to install solar panels for renewable energy. Turf roofs insulate, make up for lost ground and provide the local wildlife with a new habitat. Even the cleaning products used on site are non-toxic, eco-friendly, bulk-ordered and decanted into refillable bottles. Guests who stay here are invited to make their own considered pledge to support conservation efforts and reduce their carbon footprint.

Located in a part of the country between the sea and wild hills, the retreats are surrounded by nature, with footpaths leading from the door down to the shoreline. Noise pollution is low aside from the sounds of neighbouring farm animals. This area of Wales is an International Dark Sky Reserve, so there are amazing stargazing opportunities, with many constellations and the Milky Way all clearly in view. The retreats are the perfect excuse to down tools and devices, offering a chance to detach from daily routines. Guests can bond with the most basic of elements: fresh air, water, fire and the earth.

The cabins' decor is purposefully simple, pared back and functional. Natural materials provide a muted backdrop, with pops of colour taken from an earthy, greenery-inspired palette. Everything that anyone needs to enjoy their stay is provided and unnecessary clutter removed. Comfort comes from cosy textures and heat and light from campfires, lamps and candles. There is the chance to experience outdoor living on every level. Hammocks, hot tubs, camp stoves and wild swimming all encourage full engagement with nature.

Jessie and Lyndon have created a natural balance and bond with the landscape so that being here and breathing it all in is a restorative experience. Slow living is not only pleasurable but it also ensures the most restful night's sleep. Staying here is a chance for all the senses to absorb and be occupied in the most organic of ways. Caretaking their corner of the countryside as mindful natural mentors and custodians of their land, the new owners have made a lasting partnership with their plot.

ABOVE

A former plumber by trade in his old life in London, Lyndon put these skills to good use when creating the communal hot tubs. Warmed by a wood-fuelled stove, the hot water can be tempered with cold to get the perfect temperature. While soaking in the tubs, guests can watch the wildlife through the stable doors or above in the open sky.

RIGHT

Close to the cabin there is a natural pond where guests can enjoy wild swimming and boating. It is also a wonderful setting to engage with nature. Birds, bats, dragonflies and small mammals are all frequent visitors to the area.

OPPOSITE

A purpose-built outdoor kitchen features simple cabinetry made by Pudner Payne Products using reclaimed beams from the Treberfydd House estate. The work surfaces are fashioned from reclaimed slate and the splashback is a panel of hand-painted tiles by Francis Ceramics. The under-counter curtains are easy to remove for washing. Other humble details include glass storage jars, vintage china and a large butler's sink.

RIGHT & BELOW RIGHT

The 1950s wagon has a permanent home here, with the kitchen and eating area installed nearby under an awning made by Bespoke Tents. Sally, Hugh and their guests love being able to cook outside in the warmer months. Bark flooring keeps the ground weed-free and ensures proper drainage. In the winter, a tree-hung tent protects the kitchen from the elements.

OFF-ROAD *romance*

Once a showman's home-from-home, Sally Raikes and Hugh Martineau's circus wagon travelled to all manner of places in its former life. It has now been rehomed to serve as a very special sanctuary, standing fast in the magnificent landscape of the Brecon Beacons.

After years of being on the move, sometimes it's good to put down roots. This was the case for Sally and Hugh's reclaimed carriage-turned-cabin. Despite the constant touring, its tired exterior still showed a great deal of promise. The couple knew they could turn it into a handsome and unique haven with the addition of a few practicalities to aid modern and mindful living.

Originally rescued by the founders of Baileys Home, a salvage emporium in Herefordshire, the wagon had been preserved and used as an office space.

ABOVE LEFT
Interior-design help was enlisted via expert Hilary Lowe of Damson & Slate, who gave inspired suggestions for fabrics, furnishings and original homely details.

ABOVE CENTRE
Locally felled wood fills the fuel basket and brings plenty of rustic texture.

ABOVE RIGHT
Creature comforts such as fresh towels and linens have been provided for guests. Furniture brought from the main house has found a second life in the wagon.

When the Baileys eventually put it on the market, Sally and Hugh snapped it up and brought it to their home: Treberfydd House in Wales, an estate that has been passed down through many generations of the Raikes family since the mid 19th century. Now sited on the edge of an arboretum in the grounds, the wagon has become a whimsical retreat with an interior that reflects the history of the main house together with the charm of simple country living. This connection with the woods, farmland and far-reaching highland horizons affords an appreciation of the rhythm of the natural world.

Nowadays, the wagon houses sleeping and seating accommodation for two guests in the form of a super-king-size platform bed and a banquette bench, as well as plenty of built-in storage and a wood-burning stove. The new interior, which retains some of the original architectural elements such as the wall panelling and etchings on the windows, was the perfect canvas for showcasing the distinct qualities of the family home. With this in mind, Sally turned to her good friend, the stylist and designer Hilary Lowe of Damson & Slate, for guidance to realize her vision.

OPPOSITE
The retreat's interior includes a small but charming prep and storage space, which is used for all manner of purposes. With plenty of vintage food storage tins and crocks and a tray always ready to serve, it comes in handy as a kitchen area and is the perfect place to make drinks. The broad shelves are also a useful home for linens and blankets. There is even space underneath for pets to curl up for a snooze.

On arrival, Hilary was intrigued by the carriage's history and initiated a collaborative collection of textiles for its interior with patterns inspired by the Victorian Gothic splendour of Treberfydd House. The trailing oak leaves on the curtains reference a stained-glass window, cushions/pillows were informed by a floor tile in Sally and Hugh's hallway and a rose motif from a fireplace now features on textiles in the kitchen. These new designs sit comfortably alongside humbler items. Rustic blankets are draped at the door and over the bed, everyday stoneware pots and crocks adorn shelves and cupboards, and space has been found for well-read books and family trinkets.

Outside the wagon, semi-permanent cooking and dining areas have been constructed from found and reclaimed materials to enhance the new setting while looking back to the past. The canopied kitchen is sited under ancient trees with cabinets made using old oak joists from Treberfydd farmhouse, a further smallholding on the estate. These have been topped with slate from a nearby salvage yard. A stepped pathway, made with reclaimed roof tiles from the estate, leads to new outdoor shower and bathroom areas. These were built using natural materials such as blackened larch, which alludes to the similarly named Black Mountains nearby.

OPPOSITE

The dining area includes a banquette that can double up as a bed for little ones. It has large cushions/pillows rather than full upholstery, thus allowing for flexibility and ease of movement. Some of the fabrics come from Sally's own collection, while others are from Alexander Maverick. Hilary assisted with the styling.

RIGHT

The door curtain is actually an inexpensive blanket from Narberth Antiques & Interiors. Its heavy drape covers the door and is very effective at keeping out draughts. This is a clever way to upcycle favourite throws, which can be unclipped and changed with the seasons.

"The wagon has become a whimsical retreat with an interior that reflects the history of the main house together with the charm of simple country living."

This remarkable backdrop helps to feed and nurture the reflective and restful feelings inspired by a visit to the wagon. It is an ideal place to contemplate the breathtaking landscape, the slowly turning seasons and the ever-changing weather conditions, which vary from thick-with-mist mornings to cloudless nights that attract stargazers to this Dark Sky Reserve. Opportunities are abundant to engage with both the wild and the cultivated, be it watching the end-of-day aerobatics of swallows and bats, the twinkling of constellations or the yearly cycle of farm grazing and growing.

The celebration of both the wagon's carefree former life and the grand heritage house presents an unexpected pairing of old-world charm and new-dawn calm. The retreat, brought about by a combination of chance and considered creativity, is now a happy and harmonious place to embrace and enjoy high days, holidays and home time. It is a place to cook out in the countryside, dine in the wild and sleep under the stars, where good old-fashioned fun can imbue everyday routines with a touch of magic among the meadows and mountains.

ABOVE LEFT
A small solid-fuel stove provides warmth, a place to cook and even somewhere to dry socks after long walks in the countryside. Above, a rail has been fitted for further hanging capacity. In a small space, every nook and cranny has a practical purpose.

LEFT
Outside, a shower block has been constructed by Hut Builder UK using larch wood, some of which has been blackened. The stall design enables users to have the experience of showering outdoors but with no sacrifice

of privacy and protection. The water also makes a wonderful sound when it collides with the metal screen at the back.

OPPOSITE
The bedroom area feels luxurious and is an enticing space to sleep. The platform is dressed with linens from The White Company and throws from Damson & Slate. The assortment of cushions/pillows features fabric patterns that reflect the changing seasons. It includes vintage designs, family favourites from the main house and fabrics from Morris & Co., Alexander Maverick and Sally's own collection.

FRAME *of mind*

Tired of city commuting, Sophie and Rich Vermont decided to shake things up with a country move and career change. They have now created two idyllic A-frame cabins on their Yorkshire farm for all to enjoy.

From à la mode to mucking in, Sophie and Rich left behind their jobs in the fashion industry and took on a farm on the edge of the North York Moors. Bowled over by the beauty of the setting, the couple have turned it into a one-of-a-kind guest retreat. It provides all the mindful benefits of living in the wild and some of the best views across the heart of Yorkshire.

Creating places to stay that would be out of the ordinary was a priority for the couple. For inspiration, they looked to the classic A-frame houses that can be found throughout the Great Lakes region of North America.

THIS PAGE
Based on a classic American design, the A-frame cabin pierces the sky with its roofline, but still feels grounded thanks to its wide footprint. The triangular shape assigns a larger proportion of the space to living and lounging than to sleeping.

"The finished structure stands out among the traditional stone farm buildings like a bold black shard rising up out of the landscape."

OPPOSITE

The mezzanine level is a cosy sleep zone accessed via a ladder. Underneath and to the front, the kitchen, living area and hidden bathroom provide all the essential conveniences for a comfortable stay, come rain or shine. The built-in shelving and kitchen cabinetry have been designed and made bespoke to accommodate the sloping walls. Ceramics and other decorative objects are displayed on the shelves against a dark background for a striking visual contrast.

RIGHT

At the front of the cabin, a fully glazed wall frames the spectacular view. Sophie and Rich worked with a team of local builders and carpenters to carry out the design.

BELOW RIGHT

While most of the furnishings are built in, the freestanding sofa allows for flexibility. It generally faces inward in the winter and outward during summer, but it is a well-used piece all year round. Not being fixed in place will also make it easier to refresh the upholstery as needed.

They then teamed up with the specialist company Life Space Cabins, which provided detailed technical drawings, and hired a couple of skilled joiners to bring their vision to life. The accommodation now on offer at West Cawthorne Farm includes two identical A-frame cabins, one of which is shown here. It was built from simple materials: black corrugated steel for the roof, aged Siberian larch for the external cladding and plywood panels for the interior walls. There is a kitchen and bathroom to the rear of the cabin, a living space at the front and a bedroom on the mezzanine level. The Vermonts' considered planning and the makers' careful craftsmanship can be seen in the construction, right down to the smallest details. The finished structure stands out among the traditional stone farm buildings like a bold black shard rising up out of the landscape.

The A-frame design is all about outlining the view outside, so it is a perfect fit for the countryside setting. Natural light filters in through the huge glass windows, which offer expansive vistas over the surrounding fields. As part of their commitment to rewilding and conservation, Sophie and Rich have planted hundreds of trees and created a wildflower meadow, so there is now an abundant natural habitat for animals, insects and birds.

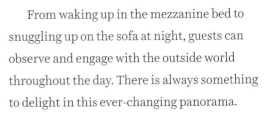

LEFT

Other freestanding furnishings in contrasting colours and textures were inspired by mid-century design or represent a fusion of Asian and Scandinavian interior styles. Here, a glossy wood table offers a sculptural partnership with a relaxed woven pouffe.

From waking up in the mezzanine bed to snuggling up on the sofa at night, guests can observe and engage with the outside world throughout the day. There is always something to delight in this ever-changing panorama.

Inside the cabin, neutral and natural tones predominate so as not to detract from the view. The look is modern rustic with an infusion of minimal Scandinavian style. The plywood panelling, which was chosen as a pared-back and inexpensive alternative to solid timber, has been treated with Osmo's wax oil in Raw Transparent for a durable, high-end finish. For contrast, the kitchen cabinetry has been coated with black paint in a flat matt finish. Rough-hewn planks salvaged from barn repairs have been repurposed as shelves, while the smart black highlights lend a contemporary edge.

Most of the furniture has been built in to make the best use of the distinctive triangular space. Bespoke joinery of this kind is well suited to unusually shaped rooms and can be surprisingly budget-friendly. Life's luxuries come in the form of ceramics from Home Barn, organic cotton bedding from Rise & Fall, uplifting toiletries from Plum & Ashby and mineral bath salts made by Seagrown, a local company committed to sustainably grown seaweed. Ikea rugs made from biodegradable

LEFT

Although divided into a number of different zones, each cabin feels cohesive and complementary, just as Sophie and Rich envisioned from the start. This one has a lighter feel thanks to the plywood shelving, which has been oiled to match the walls, unike the black-painted version shown on page 156. A few dark accents add definition.

RIGHT

The bunk area has been designed to allow a double bed to fit neatly on the platform. A small window offers rear-aspect views and daylight. The organic cotton bedding is from Rise & Fall.

BELOW

Although compact in space, each retreat has been kitted out with neat and orderly fixtures. The couple chose a narrow but deep basin, which is mounted on the wall rather than on a pedestal, for the bathroom. A mirror above serves a practical purpose and also reflects light to create the illusion of a larger space.

and recyclable jute provide warmth underfoot and echo the colours on the walls. All these natural materials create a sense of harmony with the outside world.

The couple have also taken care of any weather worries that come with the changing seasons. Even in winter, there is warmth and comfort aplenty inside with sufficient insulation and heating. And when temperatures allow,

there is a sunken bathtub on the deck, where guests can watch the wildlife while relaxing in hot water.

Sophie and Rich have created a luxurious and unique retreat, which brings a modern slice of country life to their farm. The cabins represent a vision of cool combined with comfort, which they have been able to share, enjoy and experience with others.

LEFT

The cottage has been built on a hillside and the garden uses this to its advantage to make the most of the views. In front of the house, the garden has been landscaped into terraces and footpaths with low-level swathes of plants and flowers. Trees and shrubs are pruned back regularly so as not to obstruct the windows.

BELOW LEFT

A wood-fired range cooker/stove provides a cosy and homely touch in the kitchen as well as heating the water for the radiators and hot taps/faucets. Aside from the living-room fire, the range is the main source of heat and does all the hard work to keep the house snug and cosy.

OPPOSITE

The house has the most incredible views of the Cambrian hills and valleys, and the windows have been kept minimally dressed to frame and showcase the landscape. The couple have also arranged furniture with this in mind and there are lots of seating options close to windows that extend an invitation to stop and look out. This kitchen window also has one of the quirkier light fittings in the cottage: a reconditioned factory light, which makes a great talking point.

BORN-AGAIN *bolthole*

After a countrywide search for the perfect project, James and Raffaella Fooks-Bale were charmed by this tumbledown hillside hideaway in Wales. With lots of tender loving care, they have transformed it into the most perfectly imperfect escape.

Taking on the remote cottage as a restoration project required James and Raffaella to adopt a unique approach. Built as a farm homestead 400 years ago, the house sits proudly near the top of a slope in the Cambrian Mountains and is reached by a winding track that only agile sheep and skilful drivers can navigate. The couple soon realized that assembling all the necessary building materials on site would take ingenuity, creativity and total determination.

The ethos for the design of the cottage came from the upland location itself. Its remoteness, natural situation and local landscape all fed into how the house would look and feel. Many of the rebuilding materials — such as wood from the old pigsty and clay pipes found in the garden — came from what was already there and their aged, weather-worn finishes lent their character to the renovation. Anything that was fit for another use was embraced, resulting in sensitive additions that sit happily within their surroundings. The fabric of the building now humbly grounds itself in the landscape with stone from the hillside and reclaimed wood.

LEFT & OPPOSITE

For the best use of space, James and Rafaella have installed built-in banquette seating in the dining area (left), which is located just off the fitted kitchen (opposite). This room was carved out from an existing internal hallway and stairwell, and is well integrated into the flow of the rest of the house. This bespoke solution also offers plentiful space with a range of cupboards under the banquette, which were built on site. The kitchen cabinetry is minimal, but the textured backsplash adds character.

THIS PAGE
The couple chose a modular L-shaped sofa for the main living room, which allows for the most adaptable seating arrangements and has plenty of room to lie down and lounge by the fire. The sectional framework was brought up in pieces and put together in situ.

A row of low-level shelving allows for ample book storage that does not take over the room. It has been painted in the same colour as the walls so that the colourful volumes draw the eye. The modest height of the unit means that there is lots of wall space for James's favourite framed artworks above.

From the outset, the couple wanted the cottage to be at one with the landscape. With no man-made blot or build on the horizon, the draw of nature is a reminder of just how far away from the crowds they are when they spend time here. For this reason, every window offers some kind of encounter, be it taking in the views from the kitchen or watching the world go by as you soak in the bathtub. Even the garden room, which was built into the hillside, has visiting sheep and a trickling stream in view as you dine.

Throughout the interior, plants and botanical prints bring biophilic design benefits, and there is a sensory journey to be enjoyed, too. Light pools in through windows and skylights and flickers across the surfaces of wood, fabric and stone. Meanwhile, the sound of running water is a soothing constant. This perpetually active exchange highlights textures and touchpoints in every room, and keeps up a dialogue between indoors and out.

Personal passions such as sailing and yoga have inspired and shaped the character of the cottage, both functionally and aesthetically. There are many lessons to be learned from boatbuilding about efficient, space-saving interior design, while hobby collections have formed the basis for displays of meaningful memorabilia.

Most importantly, the cottage represents an inspiring model of how to live and give back to nature. James and Raffaella have embraced being off-grid with sustainability as the energy mainstay. Most of the power comes from solar panels connected to a battery. This renewable energy system will soon be expanded with the addition of a wind turbine, while the water is taken from the spring.

RIGHT
James's interest in boat design provided inspiration for many practical details, some of which have become eye-catching features in their own right. Here, the original copper piping to the radiators has been left exposed and a bare light bulb hangs from the ceiling. It is a no-frills but beautifully functional way of letting the workings of the house become part of the interior decor.

LEFT & BELOW LEFT
The couple embraced the stonework on the end wall of the cottage, which they have repointed so that it could be left exposed (left). It has a warm tone and a rough texture that complements the smooth surfaces seen elsewhere in the room. Locally found fossils provide grounding historical detail (below left).

RIGHT
The bed benefits from a bespoke headboard made using a panel of reclaimed boards, onto which wall lights have been mounted with the wiring hidden inside. This is a useful trick when trying to install electrical or even plumbing elements in an old building with solid walls. On top of the headboard, Raffaella and James have placed a box shelf against the wall for extra storage.

Breathable, non-toxic paints were a must and plant-based cleaning products are a feature of everyday life here. The remote location and lack of refuse collection have made the couple more mindful about waste and consumption, too. They now seek out products with less packaging and recycle as much as they can. Having spent time without heat or light during the building project means that they no longer take any resources for granted and try to make sustainable choices every day, from their decor to how they wash the dishes.

James and Raffaella are keen upcyclers and saw great potential in items they found on the property. The kitchen table came from the stable, an old animal trough is now a basin and a work surface has been made from pigsty

panelling. Even pieces of moss-covered slate and stone from outside have been repurposed as trivets for pots and pans.

The refurbishment has made many lovely memories. Long days spent finding creative solutions to DIY dilemmas were followed by equally inventive one-pot meals and then evenings illuminated by candlelight. Though the cottage is rather more comfortable nowadays, this simple way of life has an enduring appeal.

The journey to deliver James and Raffaella's country escape was not one for the faint-hearted and they were often pushed to come up with some very out-of-the-box ideas and workarounds from concept to completion. However, because they were prepared to go with the tide and only take what they need, the place has drawn them in. It allows them to live very differently from their everyday lives in London, where they both work in the busy world of branding and design. By embracing the imperfect and respecting the bones of the building, they have created a simple retreat that offers so many complex and satisfying moments of pure enjoyment.

THIS PAGE
The textured stone wall
seen in the bedroom is also
the backdrop to a double
shower enclosure in the
bathroom. Absorbing and
releasing moisture through
its porous surface, the
stone naturally supports
the indoor climate. It is
non-slip and easy to
maintain, since water either
drips away or penetrates
very slowly into the surface.

*"James and
Raffaella are keen
upcyclers and saw
great potential in
items they found
on the property."*

LEFT

As with the other rooms, the main bathroom's furniture and fittings had to be built on site. A modern and minimal tub has been boxed in with simple panelling, with the addition of stylish brushed-brass hardware. To bring a sense of individuality to the room, an old stone trough earthed up outside has been turned into a characterful basin on top of a vintage chest of drawers/dresser.

BELOW

Part of the pleasure of creating this captivating cottage was reusing the materials found already on site. Many of these have been incorporated into the structure or used as surfaces, but where James and Raffaella had the most fun was in adapting some of the existing furniture. For example, in this bedroom a large table has been cut down in size to make a small but smart desk area.

ABOVE

Throughout the project, wily and smart building solutions were frequently explored, such as this sideways tap/faucet next to another old stone basin in the smaller bathroom. Rough-hewn planking disguises the plumbing work.

SOURCES

FABRICS & TEXTILES

HUG AT HOME
hugathome.co.uk
The online retail outlet of Phoenox Texiles, which produces rugs, throws and other homewares using natural fibres and recycled plastic.

KVADRAT
kvadrat.dk
Durable, eco-friendly outdoor fabrics designed to withstand the elements and look good all year round.

PHIFER
phifer.com
Perfect for waterside and poolside upholstery, Phifer's GeoBella collection of outdoor fabrics is made from a 100% recyclable polypropylene fabric known as Olefin.

SUNBRELLA
sunbrella.com
A range of home and marine textiles to suit all outdoor uses, including some fabrics made from recycled yarn.

VYVA FABRICS
vyvafabrics.com
Vyva's eco-friendly textiles brands use materials including cork, hemp and PETA-approved vegan suede. The company's own range is called F.4.L (fabrics for life).

WEAVER GREEN
weavergreen.com
Rugs, blankets, throws and cushions/pillows made from recycled plastic bottles – some have the softness of wool in a totally waterproof weave.

SURFACES

ALUSID
alusid.co.uk
With a promise of always using at least 98% recycled materials, Alusid creates solid surfaces and tiles from discarded glass and porcelain.

BRITISH RECYCLED PLASTIC
britishrecycledplastic.co.uk
This firm's recycled plastic lumber planks are designed for quick and eco-friendly construction of boardwalks, fencing and pontoons. They are especially useful for waterside retreats and in areas that are prone to flooding.

CEMENT TILE SHOP
cementtileshop.com
Beautiful tiles made by hand using natural ingredients, perfect for indoor and outdoor use. The company is based in the US and ships around the world.

ECO OUTDOOR
ecooutdoorusa.com
This leading eco-aware wall cladding, flooring, tile and furniture company creates tough and resilient pieces using natural materials.

MANDARIN STONE
mandarinstone.com
Natural stone and ceramic flooring, tiles and pavers. There is something to suit all tastes in the varied collection.

WOODWORKS
woodworks1988.com
Antique, reclaimed and FSC-certified new wood floors from a heritage firm with headquarters in both the UK and the US.

HUTS & HIDEAWAYS

BOUTIQUE CAMPING
boutiquecamping.com
Online glamping and camping emporium for tents, shelters, stoves and accessories.

PLANKBRIDGE
plankbridge.com
Leading makers of designer shepherd's huts on wheels. The perfect extra room either close to home or in the wild.

POD SPACE
pod-space.co.uk
Contemporary and environmentally friendly modular cabins built from natural materials.

TIMBERSPECS
ecofriendlycabins.com
Design and build company making and installing eco-friendly and sustainable one- and two-storey log cabins across Europe.

WILD & COUNTRY
wildandcountry.co.uk
Builder of lodges and complementary furniture that connect people with nature.

FURNITURE & FITTINGS

ENVIROBUILD
envirobuild.com
Decking and outdoor furniture made from natural and eco-friendly materials. Conservation charities including the Rainforest Trust UK receive 10% of the company's profits.

IKEA
ikea.com
Brilliant and budget-friendly basics to create a simple retreat backdrop. Ikea's mantra is to encourage 'a sustainable everyday' with recycled and longer-life products, buy-back schemes and inspiring furniture hacks.

NKUKU
nkuku.com
Ethically produced from natural and sustainable materials, Nkuku's furniture is designed with longevity in mind.

THE OUTDOOR KITCHEN COMPANY
outdoorkitchenco.co.uk
Bespoke and environmentally conscious outdoor kitchens.

POTTERY BARN
potterybarn.com
Offering a range of sustainably sourced and artisan-made homewares, this US lifestyle store ships nationwide.

PUJI
puji.com
Considered furniture for storage, seating, lazing and dining with artisan features and natural finishes.

RH
rh.com
Unique and leading designer-maker of statement furniture and homewares.

ROCKETT ST GEORGE
rockettstgeorge.co.uk
Ethically aware and considered curator of natural, upcycled, characterful and trail-blazing furniture, homewares and accessories.

SCARAMANGA
scaramangashop.co.uk
Carefully sourced retro, vintage and restored furniture outlet offering affordable antiques.

TIKAMOON
tikamoon.com
Furniture designs made from considered and ethical natural materials.

VINTERIOR
vinterior.co
Expert-curated online vintage market showcasing all styles of antique and period furniture.

WEST ELM
westelm.com
Proud of its FSC-rated indoor and outdoor collections, this high-street favourite champions contemporary style for the modern home.

HEATING, LIGHTING & COOKING

BIG GREEN EGG
biggreenegg.co.uk
The eco-friendly choice for outdoor cooks, this egg-shaped charcoal grill is designed for stress-free roasting, baking, smoking, slow cooking and more.

CONTURA
contura.eu
Swedish manufacturer of energy-efficient and low-carbon-emitting stoves with worldwide shipping.

INDUSTVILLE
industville.co.uk
Designer-maker of artisan-crafted light fixtures made with both sustainability and style in mind.

LIGHTS4FUN
lights4fun.co.uk
With a wide range of decorative lights for indoors and out, this company leads the way with its solar-powered and LED lighting for all seasons and celebrations.

HOMEWARES, WELLBEING & WILDLIFE

ANTHROPOLOGIE
anthropologie.com
Beautiful, eclectic and eco-friendly homewares that will lend your retreat a home-from-home vibe.

CHALK & MOSS
chalkandmoss.com
This firm prides itself on being the independent choice for sustainable home accessories, including delicious scents and plastic-free purchases.

THE COASTAL LIFESTYLE COMPANY
thecoastallifestyle company.co.uk
Authentic shoreline-inspired homewares and accessories.

DESIGN VINTAGE
designvintage.co.uk
An eclectic mix of eco-chic vintage, ethnic and artisan wares.

FALCON ENAMELWARE
falconenamelware.com
Timeless and durable enamel kitchenalia and tableware with a retro style.

THE FUTURE KEPT
thefuturekept.com
Jeska and Dean Hearne sell ethically sourced sustainable and beautiful products for mindful retreat making and experiences. They donate 1% of all sales to environmental not-for-profit groups.

H&M
hm.com
Eco awareness is spread across all H&M's collections. It offers a specific Conscious Choice range comprising homewares and everyday accessories.

I GIGI
igigigeneralstore.com
Authentic and original particulars for dressing and decorating places and spaces.

MELIN TREGWYNT
melintregwynt.co.uk
Artisan designer-maker of traditional Welsh blankets, fabrics, cushions/pillows and cosy home textiles.

MERCHANTS OF THE SEA
merchantsofthesea.com
Online curiosity shop of vintage coastal-inspired finds and nautical homewares.

PROTECT THE PLANET
protecttheplanet.co.uk
Making greener and mindful choices more accessible for outdoor fun, this brand offers simple and soulful ideas and inspiration.

ZARA
zarahome.com
Producing stylish home and fashion collections with the environment in mind, Zara has introduced a Join Life label for products made with sustainable materials and practices.

PAINTS, STAINS & FINISHES

AURO
auropaint.co.uk
Natural and environmentally friendly water-based eggshell and gloss paints.

BAUWERK
bauwerkcolour.com
Modern lime paints made with natural pigments.

GRAPHENSTONE
graphenstone.co.uk
With impressive eco credentials, Graphenstone's paints offer breathable coverage for indoors and out.

LAKELAND PAINTS
lakelandpaints.co.uk
Solvent- and VOC-free paints for walls, floors, masonry and wood and metal surfaces.

LICK
lick.com
In addition to making eco-friendly paints, this brand has partnered with 4ocean to remove plastic from the seas and with the One Tree Planted reforestation programme.

ORGANOWOOD
organowood.co.uk
Natural and organic treatments for wooden furniture and buildings.

OSMO
osmouk.com
Oils and waxes for outdoor wood made with purified and refined ingredients.

TREATEX
treatex.co.uk
Wildlife-friendly stains, waxes and oils.

PICTURE CREDITS

KEY: *a* = above, *b* = below, *r* = right, *l* = left, *c* = centre

All photography by Dan Duchars

1 Pearl Beach House in Marazion, available to rent at www.mouseholeboutiquestays.com; *2* Secret Treehouse, Herefordshire, available to hire via KIP Hideaways www.kiphideaways.com; *3l* Batman's Summerhouse by www.twocabins.com; *3c* Harriet's shed in Herefordshire, @yomargey; *3r* Rest + Wild, remote cabins in Shropshire, www.restandwild.co; *5a* Tincture, available to rent through Unique Homestays www.uniquehomestays.com; *5b* Pearl Beach House in Marazion, available to rent at www.mouseholeboutiquestays.com; *6–7* Batman's Summerhouse by www.twocabins.com; *8–9* Pearl Beach House in Marazion, available to rent at www.mouseholeboutiquestays.com; *10* Tincture, available to rent through Unique Homestays www.uniquehomestays.com; *11a* Harriet's shed in Herefordshire, @yomargey; *11c* Velvet Morning and Wide Beam Barge, designed by Sam Barbic, available to rent at www.boutiquebarges.co.uk; *11b* Rest + Wild, remote cabins in Shropshire, www.restandwild.co; *12al* Secret Treehouse, Herefordshire, available to hire via KIP Hideaways www.kiphideaways.com; *12ar* Crafts Hill Barn – Unique Rural Retreats and Luxury Rustic B&B Suites for two, www.craftshillbarn.co.uk; *12b* Rest + Wild, remote cabins in Shropshire, www.restandwild.co; *13* Harriet's shed in Herefordshire, @yomargey; *14* A-frame Cabins, a luxurious and unique stay in nature, available to rent at www.northyorkshirehideaways.com; *15al* Tincture, available to rent through Unique Homestays www.uniquehomestays.com; *15ar* One Cat Farm, unique cabins in the wild www.onecatfarm.com; *15cl* Tincture, available to rent through Unique Homestays www.uniquehomestays.com; *15cr* A-frame Cabins, a luxurious and unique stay in nature, available to rent at www.northyorkshirehideaways.com; *15bl* Batman's Summerhouse by www.twocabins.com; *15br* Pearl Beach House in Marazion, available to rent at www.mouseholeboutiquestays.com; *16a & c* Secret Treehouse, Herefordshire, available to hire via KIP Hideaways www.kiphideaways.com; *16b–17* Velvet Morning and Wide Beam Barge, designed by Sam Barbic, available to rent at www.boutiquebarges.co.uk; *18* The summerhouse of Norfolk based photographer and stylist, Tamsyn Morgans; *19al* Tincture, available to rent through Unique Homestays www.uniquehomestays.com; *19ar* Secret Treehouse, Herefordshire, available to hire via KIP Hideaways www.kiphideaways.com; *19b* Batman's Summerhouse by www.twocabins.com; *20* One Cat Farm, unique cabins in the wild www.onecatfarm.com; *21a* Crafts Hill Barn –Unique Rural Retreats and Luxury Rustic B&B Suites for two, www.craftshillbarn.co.uk; *21c* Molly's Wagon at Treberfydd, Powys, available to rent. See www.treberfydd.com for details; *21b* Pearl Beach House in Marazion, available to rent at www.mouseholeboutiquestays.com; *22* Molly's Wagon at Treberfydd, Powys, available to rent. See www.treberfydd.com for details; *23al* Pearl Beach House in Marazion, available to rent at www.mouseholeboutiquestays.com; *23ar* Secret Treehouse, Herefordshire, available to hire via KIP Hideaways www.kiphideaways.com; *23bl* Pearl Beach House in Marazion, available to rent at www.mouseholeboutiquestays.com; *23br* Harriet's shed in Herefordshire, @yomargey; *24* Tincture, available to rent through Unique Homestays www.uniquehomestays.com; *25al* Secret Treehouse, Herefordshire, available to hire via KIP Hideaways www.kiphideaways.com; *25ar* Velvet Morning and Wide Beam Barge, designed by Sam Barbic, available to rent at www.boutiquebarges.co.uk; *25bl* Molly's Wagon at Treberfydd, Powys, available to rent. See www.treberfydd.com for details; *25br* Secret Treehouse, Herefordshire, available to hire via KIP Hideaways www.kiphideaways.com; *26a* Rest + Wild, remote cabins in Shropshire, www.restandwild.co; *26c* Velvet Morning and Wide Beam Barge, designed by Sam Barbic, available to rent at www.boutiquebarges.co.uk; *26b* Tincture, available to rent through Unique Homestays www.uniquehomestays.com; *27* Rest + Wild, remote cabins in Shropshire, www.restandwild.co; *28* Crafts Hill Barn – Unique Rural Retreats and Luxury Rustic B&B Suites for two, www.craftshillbarn.co.uk; *29a* One Cat Farm, unique cabins in the wild www.onecatfarm.com; *29bl* Batman's Summerhouse by www.twocabins.com; *29br* Harriet's shed in Herefordshire, @yomargey; *30al* Secret Treehouse, Herefordshire, available to hire via KIP Hideaways www.kiphideaways.com; *30ar* Tincture, available to rent through Unique Homestays www.uniquehomestays.com; *30cl & bl* Velvet Morning and Wide Beam Barge, designed by Sam Barbic, available to rent at www.boutiquebarges.co.uk; *30cr* Tincture, available to rent through Unique Homestays www.uniquehomestays.com; *30br* Pearl Beach House in Marazion, available to rent at www.mouseholeboutiquestays.com; *32* Velvet Morning and Wide Beam Barge, designed by Sam Barbic, available to rent at www.boutiquebarges.co.uk; *33a* Rest + Wild, remote cabins in Shropshire, www.restandwild.co; *33c* Harriet's shed in Herefordshire, @yomargey; *33b* A-frame Cabins, a luxurious and unique stay in nature, available to rent at www.northyorkshirehideaways.com; *34al* The summerhouse of Norfolk based photographer and stylist, Tamsyn Morgans; *34ar* Batman's Summerhouse by www.twocabins.com; *34bl* Crafts Hill Barn – Unique Rural Retreats and Luxury Rustic B&B Suites for two, www.craftshillbarn.co.uk; *34br* Pearl Beach House in Marazion, available to rent at www.mouseholeboutiquestays.com; *35* Velvet Morning and Wide Beam Barge, designed by Sam Barbic, available to rent at www.boutiquebarges.co.uk; *36al* Velvet Morning and Wide Beam Barge, designed by Sam Barbic, available to rent at www.boutiquebarges.co.uk; *36bl* Tincture, available to rent through Unique Homestays www.uniquehomestays.com; *37* Batman's Summerhouse by www.twocabins.com; *38a & b* Secret Treehouse, Herefordshire, available to hire via KIP Hideaways www.kiphideaways.com; *38c & 39* Batman's Summerhouse by www.twocabins.com; *40* One Cat Farm, unique cabins in the wild www.onecatfarm.com; *41al* Batman's Summerhouse by www.twocabins.com; *41ar* Tincture, available to rent through Unique Homestays www.uniquehomestays.com; *41bl* Harriet's shed in Herefordshire, @yomargey; *41br* Pearl Beach House in Marazion, available to rent at www.mouseholeboutiquestays.com; *42* One Cat Farm, unique cabins in the wild, www.onecatfarm.com; *43a* Harriet's shed in Herefordshire, @yomargey; *43c* Secret Treehouse, Herefordshire, available to hire via KIP Hideaways www.kiphideaways.com; *43b* Crafts Hill Barn – Unique Rural Retreats and Luxury Rustic B&B Suites for two, www.craftshillbarn.co.uk; *44* Molly's Wagon at Treberfydd, Powys, available to rent. See www.treberfydd.com for details; *45a* Crafts Hill Barn – Unique Rural Retreats and Luxury Rustic B&B Suites for two, www.craftshillbarn.co.uk; *45bl* Velvet Morning and Wide Beam Barge, designed by Sam Barbic, available to rent at www.boutiquebarges.co.uk; *45br* Tincture, available to rent through Unique Homestays www.uniquehomestays.com; *46* Crafts Hill Barn – Unique Rural Retreats and Luxury Rustic B&B Suites for two, www.craftshillbarn.co.uk; *47* Harriet's shed in Herefordshire, @yomargey; *48–55* The summerhouse of Norfolk based photographer and stylist, Tamsyn Morgans; *66–73* Harriet's shed in Herefordshire, @yomargey; *74–79* Crafts Hill Barn – Unique Rural Retreats and Luxury Rustic B&B Suites for two, www.craftshillbarn.co.uk; *80–91* Pearl Beach House in Marazion, available to rent at www.mouseholeboutiquestays.com; *92–97* Crafts Hill Barn – Unique Rural Retreats and Luxury Rustic B&B Suites for two, www.craftshillbarn.co.uk; *98–113* Velvet Morning and Wide Beam Barge, designed by Sam Barbic, available to rent at www.boutiquebarges.co.uk; *114–121* Batman's Summerhouse by www.twocabins.com; *122–133* Secret Treehouse, Herefordshire, available to hire via KIP Hideaways www.kiphideaways.com; *134–139* Rest + Wild, remote cabins in Shropshire, www.restandwild.co; *140–145* One Cat Farm, unique cabins in the wild www.onecatfarm.com; *146–153* Molly's Wagon at Treberfydd, Powys, available to rent. See www.treberfydd.com for details; *154–159* A-frame Cabins, a luxurious and unique stay in nature, available to rent at www.northyorkshirehideaways.com; *160–169* Tincture, available to rent through Unique Homestays www.uniquehomestays.com; *173* Secret Treehouse, Herefordshire, available to hire via KIP Hideaways www.kiphideaways.com; *174 & 176* Tincture, available to rent through Unique Homestays www.uniquehomestays.com.

BUSINESS CREDITS

KEY: *a* = above, *b* = below, *l* = left, *c* = centre, *r* = right.

BATMAN'S SUMMERHOUSE
www.twocabins.com
and
Miranda Gardiner Paintings
www.mirandagardiner.co.uk
with
ceramics by Pippi & Me
www.pippiandmeceramics.com
3l; 6–7; 15bl; 19b; 29bl; 34ar; 37; 38c; 39; 41al; 114–121.

CABIN DESIGNED & BUILT BY DAVE COOTE & ATLANTA BARTLETT
www.paleandinteresting.com
and
Marysia Lachowicz
Visual Artist
www.marysia.co.uk
4; 31; 36ar; 56–65.

CRAFTS HILL BARN
www.craftshillbarn.co.uk
and
Wooden products (breadboard, stools and benches) by Idea Tree Designs
www.ideatreedesigns.com
12ar; 21c; 28; 34bl; 43b; 45a; 46; 74–79; 92–97.

HARRIET THISTLEWAYTE
@yomargey
3c; 11 a; 13; 23br; 29br; 33c; 41bl; 43a; 47; 66–73.

KIP HIDEAWAYS
www.kiphideaways.com
and
Interiors by Harriet Churchward
Built by Matt Pescod
Architecture by William Millward Architecture
2; 12al; 16a; 16c; 19ar; 23ar; 25al; 30al; 38a; 38b; 43c; 122–133; 173.

ONE CAT FARM
www.onecatfarm.com
15ar; 20; 29a; 40; 42; 140–145.

PEARL BEACH HOUSE
Available to rent for getaways and as a film/television location
www.mouseholeboutiquestays.com
1; 5b; 8–9; 15br; 21b; 23al; 23bl; 30br; 34br; 41br; 80–91.

REST + WILD
www.restandwild.co
3r; 11b; 12b; 26a; 27; 33a; 134–139.

SALLY RAIKES
Treberfydd House
Llangasty
Brecon LD3 7PX.
www.treberfydd.com
and
Pudner & Payne
E: pudnerpayneproducts@gmail.com
21c; 22; 25bl; 44; 146–153.

SAM BARBIC
Designer
www.sambarbic.co.uk
and
Boutique Barges
www.boutiquebarges.co.uk
11c; 16b; 17; 25ar; 26c; 30cl; 30bl; 32; 35; 36al; 45bl; 98–113.

TAMSYN MORGANS
Photographer and Stylist
www.tamsynmorgans.com
@tamsynmorgans
18; 34 al; 48–58.

UNIQUE HOMESTAYS
www.uniquehomestays.com
T: +44 (0)1637 881183
5a; 10; 15al; 15cl; 19al; 24; 26b; 30ar; 30cr; 36bl; 41ar; 45br; 160–169; 174; 176.

A-FRAME CABINS & THE BARNS
West Cawthorne Farm
Cawthorne
Pickering YO18 8EH.
Available to rent at
www.northyorkshirehideaways.com
and
A-Frame cabin architects:
Life Space Cabins
Moorshead Sawmills
Yealmpton
Devon PL8 2ES
www.lifespacecabins.co.uk
and
A-frame construction:
MDB Joinery
@mdbjoinery
and
RAS Joinery
@ras_joinery
14; 15cr; 33b; 154–159.

INDEX

Page numbers in *italic* refer to the illustrations

ACKNOWLEDGEMENTS

In making this book, we'd like to thank many kind and thoughtful people who have helped us along the way, beginning with the fantastic team at Ryland Peters & Small. They have offered us such wonderful support once again on this publication and we are so incredibly proud to work with them.

Thanks, too, to the delightful retreat owners who graciously invited us in to see and share their beautiful sanctuaries and get-away spaces. It was a very special honour to hear their heartfelt stories of how each one came about and how it is used today.

To our followers, we thank you for your compassionate comments and conversations. Please do carry on sharing and sending your thoughts, ideas and hashtags. Find us on Instagram and Facebook @thecontentednest #retreatsforthesoul. Finally, much love and gratitude go to our friends and family, who continue to encourage us.

The story of why, how, and where we create a retreat is such a personal matter and journey. Sometimes a life-changing proposal begins with a definite design, while at other times it is an organic process from the off. Each considered creative stage adds a mutually beneficial layer of satisfaction as an idea takes shape: simple, smart, soulful and sustainable. We dedicate this book to the next generation of haven makers. May you find that fulfilment as you craft your own hideaway space.

With love
Sara and Dan
The CONTENTed Nest